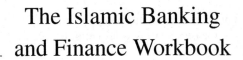

The Islamic Banking
and Finance Workbook

The Islamic Banking and Finance Workbook

Step-by-Step Exercises to Help You Master the Fundamentals of Islamic Banking and Finance

Brian Kettell

A John Wiley and Sons, Ltd., Publication

This edition first published in 2011
© 2011 Brian Kettell

Registered office
John Wiley & Sons Ltd, The Atrium, Southern Gate, Chichester, West Sussex, PO19 8SQ, United Kingdom

For details of our global editorial offices, for customer services and for information about how to apply for permission to reuse the copyright material in this book please see our website at www.wiley.com.

ISBN 978-0-470-97805-4 (paperback)
ISBN 978-1-119-99062-8 (ebook)
ISBN 978-1-119-99063-5 (ebook)
ISBN 978-1-119-99126-7 (ebook)

A catalogue record for this book is available from the British Library.

Typeset in 10/12pt Times by Aptara Inc., New Delhi, India
Printed in Great Britain by CPI Antony Rowe, Chippenham, Wiltshire

To my wife Nadia, our son Alexei and daughter Anna. Nadia keeps the whole fleet on an even keel with only the occasional shipwreck.

Contents

Preface

The ongoing turbulence in the global financial markets has drawn attention to an alternative system of financial intermediation: Islamic banking and finance. This sector is now one of the fastest growing within the marketplace and has, so far, remained on the sidelines of this financial unrest. Since the inception of Islamic banking, about three decades ago, the number and reach of Islamic financial institutions worldwide has risen significantly. Institutions offering Islamic financial services constitute a significant and growing share of the financial system in several countries.

Indeed the Islamic finance industry is in the midst of a phenomenal expansionary phase, exhibiting average annual growth rates of about 15% in recent years. This rapid growth has been fuelled not only by a surging demand for *Sharia'a*-compliant products from financiers in the Middle East and Muslim countries, but also by investors around the world, thus rendering the expansion of Islamic finance a global phenomenon.

Besides its wide geographical scope, the rapid expansion of Islamic finance is also taking place across the whole spectrum of financial activities, ranging from retail banking to insurance and capital market investments. But perhaps the most striking has been the fast growth of *sukuk* (Islamic bonds), the most popular form of securitised credit finance within the industry. *Sukuk* issuance soared over the period 2001–2007 although it has fallen back more recently.

Educational and training material for the industry is, however, lagging far behind the speed at which the industry is evolving. Indeed the lack of quality educational and training material has now become a serious obstacle to effective training and education. This workbook is designed to provide students and practitioners with the *first ever workbook* that enables readers to test their understanding of the underlying principles. Emphasis is placed on multiple choice questions and tests of the basic concepts. Suggested answers are provided.

It must be stressed that the newness of the industry means that designing quality educational and training material is fraught with problems. In addition to this newness the industry also faces the challenge of changing *Sharia'a* interpretations of many of the products. Although this factor should not be exaggerated, given that *Sharia'a* law has been around for centuries, the existence of different schools of Islamic jurisprudence (*Fiqh*) combined with controversies revolving around some of the contracts has certainly created some uncertainties as to how the contracts are being applied.

These aspects may lead to the potential for controversy over some of my suggested answers. No doubt some of the answers will be disputed. I cannot claim to have universal answers and would ask that readers please assume that these may change over time.

If readers do feel strongly that they have an alternative answer I would certainly welcome a dialogue. Indeed if anyone wishes to provide me with reasons for their proposed alternative solutions I would urge them to please do so, and I will be delighted to thank them in later editions. It is this dialogue that is so important for the health and future of the industry and I look forward to an active debate with the readers. My email address is brian.kettell@islamicbankingcourses.com.

Companion texts are available from the publishers: *Introduction to Islamic Banking and Finance* **and** *Case Studies in Islamic Banking and Finance*.

About the Author

Brian Kettell has a wealth of practical experience in the area of Islamic banking and finance. He worked for several years as an Advisor for the Central Bank of Bahrain where he had numerous Islamic banking responsibilities.

Subsequently, Brian taught courses on Islamic banking and finance at a range of financial institutions including the World Bank, National Commercial Bank (Saudi Arabia), Global Investment House (Kuwait), Noor Islamic Bank (UAE), the UK Treasury, the Central Bank of Iran, the Central Bank of Syria, the Chartered Institute for Securities and Investment, the Institute for Financial Services and Scotland Yard.

Brian's vast academic expertise in Islamic finance is highlighted by his role as former Joint Editor of the *Islamic Finance Qualification Handbook* and his past teaching work at a number of top universities worldwide including the London School of Economics, the City University of Hong Kong, the American University of the Middle East in Kuwait and London Metropolitan University Business School.

Brian's impressive list of publications include over 100 articles in journals, business magazines and the financial press including *Islamic Business and Finance*, *Islamic Banking and Finance*, the *Central Banking Journal*, *Euromoney*, the *Securities Journal* and the *International Currency Review*. He has also published 16 books on Islamic banking and financial markets.

1
What Do You Know About Islam?

1.1 LEARNING OUTCOMES, SUMMARY OVERVIEW AND PROBLEMS

1.1.1 Learning Outcomes

After reading Chapter 1 you should be able to do the following:

- Describe the role played in Islam by the Prophet Mohammed.
- Explain the Islamic five pillars of faith.
- Describe *zakat*.
- Define the Islamic creed.
- Explain how one becomes a Muslim.
- Distinguish *zakat* from *sadaqah*.
- Describe *Salat*.
- Explain the Islamic belief in angels.
- Describe the *hajj*.
- Explain the Islamic belief in *Qada'ar*.
- Describe the *Shahada*.
- Explain the Islamic belief in the Apostles.
- Define the *Ulema*.
- Explain the importance of Ramadan to Muslims.
- Describe *Tawhid*.
- Define *imam*.
- Contrast the *hajj* with the *umra*.
- Explain the Islamic belief in the Hereafter.
- Explain the Islamic belief in the revealed Books.
- Test that you have fully understood the Islam beliefs that drive Islamic banking.

1.1.2 Summary Overview

The books of the Islamic faith shape both the culture and philosophy of the Muslim world.

1.1.2.1 The Books of Islam

- **The *Qur'an*:** For Muslims, the *Qur'an* is the 'Word of God'. Muslims believe the identical book is in Heaven and Allah sent the angel Gabriel to Mohammed to reveal his 'Word'. The *Qur'an* is divided into 114 chapters or *Surahs*. These *Surahs* are revelations given to Mohammed during his 23 years of 'Prophethood' from AD 610 to 632.

  The *Qur'an*, composed during Mohammed's lifetime, corresponds to the time and circumstances of his life. The *Surahs* can be divided into three time periods. The earliest are the shortest and known as *Early Meccan*, and date from AD 610 to 622. These were composed in Mecca, prior to the Hegira where Mohammed fled to Medina in September AD 622.

The *Median Surahs* were composed during the time when Muslims controlled the city of Medina. They date from AD 622 to 630.

The *Late Meccan Surahs* were written between AD 630 and 632, during the last two years of Mohammed's life and after Mecca surrendered to his authority.

At this time, *Surahs* were not collected in one book but were memorised and collated on various items. The *Hafiz* were Muslims who had committed much of the *Qur'an* to memory. In the battle of Yamamah in AD 633, many of the Hafiz died.

With the urging of Umar, Zayd ibn Thabit, one of Mohammed's most trusted secretaries, was appointed to the task of collecting the *Qur'an* into one book. Still later, after different versions of the *Qur'an* began to appear, Zayd was put in charge of collecting all the *Qur'ans* throughout the Muslim world and issuing an authorised copy in the place of the one's collected.

- **The *Hadith*:** After the death of Mohammed, his followers collected his sayings and actions in books to guide and direct their beliefs. They gave additional meaning behind the *Surahs* and helped interpret their meanings. The most respected *Hadith* are the collected works of *Bukari*. Muslims do not feel that the *Hadith* is the 'Word of God'. They would compare the *Hadith* to the Christian Gospels, which report what Jesus said.

1.1.2.2 Who is a Muslim?

A Muslim is someone who submits to Allah by confession of the *Shahada*, which is part of the five pillars of faith – observances in Islam that are foundational practices, or duties, that every Muslim must observe:

- **The Five Pillars of Faith:**
  - 1. The Confession: 'La ilaha illa llah' ('There is no God but God'); the *Shahada* (testimony); the *Kalima* ('There is no God but Allah, and Mohammed is the Prophet of Allah').
  - 2. *Salat* (prayer) five times a day facing Mecca.
  - 3. *Zakat* (almsgiving).
  - 4. Fasting during the month of Ramadan, from sunrise until sundown.
  - 5. *Hajj*: pilgrimage to Mecca once in a lifetime.

In addition, there are five major beliefs or doctrines in Islam:

- **The Five Articles of Faith:**
  - 1. *God*: There is only one true God and his name is Allah. Allah is all knowing, all-powerful and sovereign judge. Yet Allah is not a personal God, for he is so far above humans in every way that he is not personally knowable.
  - 2. *Angels*: Angels in Islam serve Allah's will, as with Gabriel delivering the *Qur'an* to Mohammed. Angels do not perform any bodily functions (sexual, eating and so on) because they are created from light. Angels serve different purposes. Each person has two recording angels who record his or her good or bad deeds.
  - 3. *Scripture*: There are four inspired books in Islam: *Qur'an*, Torah (the 'Books of Moses', Ingil (Gospel of Jesus) and Zabur (Psalms of David). These are the books mentioned in the *Qur'an* as God's Word, but most Muslims feel the latter three books are corrupt. For this reason Allah, gave Mohammed the '*Qur'an*'.

- 4. *Prophets*: In Islam God has spoken through numerous prophets down through the centuries, including Adam, Noah, Abraham, Moses and Jesus. The greatest prophet and the last prophet is Mohammed; he is the seal of the prophets.
- 5. *Last Days*: The last days will be a time of Resurrection and judgement. Everybody will be resurrected to stand before Allah to be judged on the Last Day. Those who follow Allah and Mohammed will go to Paradise. Others will go to Hell.

1.2   QUESTIONS

1. What does Islam mean?

   _____

   _____

   _____

   _____

2. Muslims make no distinction between

   A:_____

   _____

   B:_____

   _____

3. A Muslim is

   A:_____

   _____

   B:_____

   _____

4. How does one become a Muslim?

   _____

   _____

   _____

   _____

5. What are the two main sects within Islam?

   A:_____

   _____

   B:_____

   _____

6. What are the similarities between *Shia* Islam and *Sunni* Islam?

    _____

    _____

    _____

7. What are the differences between *Shiites* and *Sunnis*?

    Shiites believe:_____

    _____

    Sunnis believe:_____

    _____

8. List the Five Pillars of Islam.

    A:_____

    _____

    B:_____

    _____

    C:_____

    _____

    D:_____

    _____

    E:_____

9. What are the principal sources of the *Sharia'a*?

    A:_____

    _____

    B:_____

    _____

    C:_____

    _____

    D:_____

    _____

10. Give four examples of Islamic investment principles.

    A:_____

    _____

✐B:_____

_____

✐C:_____

_____

✐D:_____

_____

11. What are the six doctrines of the Islamic creed?

✐A:_____

_____

✐B:_____

_____

✐C:_____

_____

✐D:_____

_____

✐E:_____

_____

✐F:_____

_____

In the following questions, only one statement is true. Please indicate the letter of the true statement.

12. Which of the following is true?
    A. Islam is the world's largest religion.
    B. Islam is the world's second largest religion.
    C. Islam is the world's third largest religion.

13. Where did Islam begin?
    A. In modern-day Jerusalem.
    B. In modern-day Saudi Arabia.
    C. In modern-day Egypt.

14. What does it take to convert to being a Muslim?
    A. You can't readily. You are either born into the faith or, in limited circumstances, become a Muslim by marriage.
    B. Personal study and preparation during one Islamic year, mentored by two practising Muslims and a sponsoring *imam*.
    C. Making the declaration of faith, in Arabic and before witnesses: 'There is no God but Allah and Mohammed is his messenger.'

15. Muslims are expected to put their faith into action through the 'five pillars of Islam'. One of them, *zakat*, is
    A. The obligation to give annually to charity.
    B. The obligation to seek potential converts.
    C. The obligation to learn the *Qur'an* by heart.
16. Which of the following statements is false?
    A. An *imam* is a quasi-political leader whose decisions are acted upon by his followers.
    B. *Jihad* describes the experience of Muslims 'struggling' to live out their faith to the best of their ability.
    C. A *Fatwa* is a legal opinion put forward by an Islamic scholar.
17. Islam was founded by
    A. Mohammed.
    B. Allah.
    C. Adam.
18. *Sunni* is to *Shia* as. . .
    A. Catholic is to Protestant.
    B. Christianity is to Judaism.
    C. Sikhism is to Hinduism.
19. What does the term the *Ummah* refer to?
    A. The Grand Mosque in Mecca.
    B. The Islamic community.
    C. Fasting at Ramadan.
20. Which of these specialises in 'law' rather than in theology?
    A. The *Imam*.
    B. The *Mufti*.
    C. The *Sheikh*.
    D. The *Muezzin*.
21. The difference between *Sunni* and *Shia* Islam is
    A. A doctrinal difference on the meaning of Allah.
    B. A political disagreement on the issue of leadership.
    C. A disagreement about the role of the prophet Mohammed.
    D. A disagreement about how battles should be waged.
22. The word 'Islam' means
    A. Justice and peace.
    B. Peace achieved through submission to Allah.
    C. Peace achieved through submission to the Prophet's message.
    D. The spread of peace around the world.
23. What do Muslims believe regarding the Prophet Mohammed?
    A. He is God.
    B. He is the son of God.
    C. He was the first Messenger from Allah sent to mankind.
    D. He was the last Messenger from Allah sent to mankind.
24. Which of the following is a prophet in Islam?
    A. Moses.
    B. Abraham.
    C. Jesus.

D. Noah.

E. All of the above are prophets.

25. The word 'Allah' means

A. Father, in Arabic.

B. The prophet of Islam.

C. The Moon God worshipped by Muslims.

D. God, in Arabic.

26. The country with the largest Muslim population is

A. Iran.

B. Pakistan.

C. Egypt.

D. Indonesia.

E. Saudi Arabia.

27. What do Muslims believe about Jesus?

A. He is a prophet who will accompany Allah on the Day of Judgement.

B. He was the result of a virgin birth.

C. He was the son of Allah.

D. He is a figure who died for the sins of mankind.

28. As reported in the *Qur'an*, the first user of the words 'Islam' and 'Muslims' was

A. Abraham.

B. Adam.

C. Mohammed.

D. Allah.

29. Which story is not in the *Qur'an*?

A. Adam and Eve.

B. Abraham's sacrifice of his son.

C. Noah's ark.

D. The crucifixion of Jesus.

30. The word *Jihad* means

A. The physical struggle necessary to make Islam the world's dominant religion.

B. Holy war.

C. To struggle and strive to practise Islam.

D. Victory for a Muslim against a non-Muslim.

31. Muslims worship

A. The *Qur'an*.

B. The *Kaaba*.

C. Mohammed.

D. Allah.

32. Under which of these names is Jesus known to Muslims?

A. Yunus.

B. Nuh.

C. Isa.

D. Azrael.

33. In contrast to *Sunnis*, *Shiites* do not believe in the *Sunnah*:

A. True.

B. False.

1.3 ANSWERS

1. Submission to the Will of God. Derived from *Aslama* – to give oneself to God.
2. Religious World and the Temporal World.
3. One who submits to Allah and can recite the *Shahada* – 'There is no God but Allah and Mohammed is Allah's Prophet'.
4. By reciting the *Shahada*.
5. *Sunni* Islam (90%) and *Shia* Islam (10%).
6. Similarities are belief in the *Qur'an*, the five pillars of Islam and the Islamic creed.
7. Differences are based on who should be the Caliph following the death of the prophet Mohammed. *Shia* Islam believes it should be a lineal descendant of Ali, the cousin and son in law of Mohammed. *Sunni* Islam believes that any righteous Muslim can be elected as Caliph.
8. A. *Shahada* – profession of faith.
   B. *Salat* – ritual prayer five times a day.
   C. *Zakat* – Islamic tax to be given to charity.
   D. Ramadan – abstention from food, drink and so on during daylight hours in the ninth month.
   E. *Hajj* – pilgrimage to Mecca.
9. A. *Qur'an* – revelation to the Prophet Mohammed.
   B. *Sunnah* and *Hadith*.
   C. *Ijma* – consensus.
   D. *Qiyas* – analogical deduction.
10. A. No interest (*riba*) is allowed.
    B. Risk sharing.
    C. Asset-backed activities.
    D. *Haram* activities.
11. A. One God – Allah.
    B. Existence of angels.
    C. Scripture revealed by Allah.
    D. Message of Allah, the Prophet Mohammed who was sent to all people.
    E. Day of Judgement.
    F. Predestination.
12. B
13. B
14. C
15. A
16. A
17. A
18. A
19. B
20. B
21. B
22. B
23. D
24. E
25. D

26. D
27. A
28. A
29. D
30. C
31. D
32. C
33. B

2

Sources of *Sharia'a* Law and the Role of *Sharia'a* Boards

2.1 LEARNING OUTCOMES, SUMMARY OVERVIEW AND PROBLEMS

2.1.1 Learning Outcomes

After reading Chapter 2 you should be able to do the following:

- Explain the role of Allah as the law giver.
- Define the *Sharia'a*.
- Describe the sources of *Sharia'a* law.
- Explain *Ijtihad*.
- Describe the role of the *Qur'an* within Islam.
- Define *Qiyas*.
- Describe the role of the *Hadith* within Islam.
- Contrast the role of the *Qur'an* and the *Hadith* within Islam.
- Define the *Sunnah*.
- Distinguish *Qiyas* from *Ijma*.
- Describe the role of promises within the *Sharia'a*.
- Define *Ijma*.
- Contrast the *Qur'an* with the *Sunnah* within the *Sharia'a*.
- Describe the role and importance of *Sharia'a* Supervisory Boards.
- Describe the role of the *Sharia'a* Supervisory Board within an Islamic financial institution.
- Test that you have fully understood the principles of *Sharia'a* law that drive Islamic banking and finance.

2.1.2 Summary Overview

According to Muslims, *Sharia'a* law is founded on the words of Allah as revealed in the *Qur'an*, and traditions (*ahadith*) gathered from the life of the Prophet Mohammed. Mohammed was born c. AD 570 in Mecca, a trading city in the Arabian desert. In addition to being a centre of trade on the caravan routes, Mecca was a place of pilgrimage for Arabs of many beliefs. The focus of religion in Mecca was the *Ka'aba*, a stone building believed to have been built by Adam at the beginning of time, and rebuilt by the Prophet Abraham and his son Ishmael.

Mecca was inhabited by the *Quraysh*, a pagan tribe with some Jews and Christians among them. Mohammed was orphaned at an early age, and came under the protection of an uncle. He grew up to become a trader and married his employer, a prosperous merchant named *Khadija*. It was in middle age that Mohammed began to speak of revelations received from Allah through the angel Gabriel. Mohammed told others of his revelations, and attracted followers who transcribed them onto available materials. In the 20 years following his first revelation until his death, Islam became the dominant force in the Arabian peninsula, and a serious challenge to the Byzantine and Sasanian empires.

After Mohammed's death, the revelations were collected and organised into the *Qur'an*, and accounts of his life eventually formed the basis for the *Sunnah*.

In pre-Islamic Arabia, bonds of common ancestry formed the basis for tribal association. The advent of Islam brought the tribes together under a single religion. As Islam is not just a religion, but also a way of life, a new common basis of law and personal behaviour, *Sharia'a*, began to take shape.

Sharia'a continued to undergo fundamental changes, beginning with the reigns of caliphs Abu Bakr (632–634) and Umar (634–644), during which time many questions were brought to the attention of Mohammed's closest comrades for consultation. During the reign of Muawiya (b. Abu Sufyan ibn Harb, c. 662), Islam undertook an urban transformation, raising questions not originally covered by Islamic law. Since then, changes in Islamic society have played an ongoing role in developing *Sharia'a*.

Sharia'a, which means 'way or path', is the sacred law of Islam. All Muslims believe that *Sharia'a* is God's law, but differences exist between groups as to exactly what it entails. Modernists, traditionalists and fundamentalists all hold varying views of *Sharia'a*, as do adherents to different schools of Islamic thought and jurisprudence. Different countries and cultures also have different interpretations of *Sharia'a*.

Muslims believe that all *Sharia'a* is derived from two primary sources: the divine revelations set forth in the *Qur'an*, and the sayings and example set by the Prophet Mohammed in the *Sunnah*. *Fiqh* (jurisprudence) interprets and extends the application of *Sharia'a* to questions not directly addressed in these primary sources, by including secondary sources. These secondary sources usually include the consensus of the religious scholars embodied in *Ijma*, and analogy from the *Qur'an* and *Sunnah* through *Qiyas*.

Where it enjoys official status, *Sharia'a* is applied by Islamic judges, or *Qadis*.

The *imam* has varying responsibilities depending on the interpretation of *Sharia'a*. Although the term is commonly used to refer to the leader of communal prayers, the *imam* may also be a scholar, religious leader or political leader.

Sharia'a deals with many topics addressed by secular law, including crime, politics and economics, as well as personal matters such as sexuality, hygiene, diet, prayer and fasting.

2.1.2.1 *Traditional Perspectives on* Sharia'a

The majority of Muslims regard themselves as belonging to either the *Sunni* or *Shia* sect of Islam. Within these sects, there are different schools of religious study and jurisprudence. The schools within each sect have common characteristics, although each differs in its details.

The Sunni *Perspective*

In addition to the 'Basic Code' of the *Qur'an* and *Sunnah*, traditional *Sunni* Muslims also add the consensus (Ijma) of Mohammed's companions (Sahaba) and Islamic Jurists (*Ulema*) on certain issues. In situations where no concrete rule exists in the sources, law scholars use *Qiy*as – various forms of reasoning, including analogy – to derive law from the essence of divine principles and preceding rulings. The consensus of the community, public interest and other sources are used as an adjunct to *Sharia'a* where the primary and secondary sources allow. This description can be applied to the major schools of *Sunni Fiqh*, which include the *Hanafi, Shafii, Maliki* and *Hanbali*.

The Shia *Perspective*

Shia Muslims also extend the 'Basic Code' with *Fiqh*, but strongly reject analogy (*Qiyas*) as an easy way to innovations (*bid'ah*), and reject consensus (*Ijma*) as not having any particular value in its own right.

During the period that the *Sunni* scholars developed those two tools, the *Shia imams* were alive, and *Shia* view them as an extension of the *Sunnah*, and so they view themselves as deriving their laws (*Fiqh*) only from the *Qur'an* and *Sunnah*.

In *Imami-Shii* law, the sources of law (*usul al-fiqh*) are the *Qur'an*, anecdotes of Mohammed's practices and those of The Twelve Imams, and the intellect ('aql). The practices called *Sharia'a* today, however, also have roots in comparative law and local customs (urf).

Shia Jurists replace *Qiyas* analogy with *'aql* (reason).

Most *Shia* Muslims follow the *Jaafari* school of thought.

Muslim countries including Pakistan, Indonesia, Afghanistan, Egypt, Nigeria, Sudan, Morocco and Malaysia have legal systems strongly influenced by *Sharia'a*, but also cede ultimate authority to their constitutions and the rule of law. These countries conduct elections, although some are also under the influence of authoritarian leaders. In these countries, politicians and Jurists make law, rather than religious scholars. Most of these countries have modernised their laws and now have legal systems with significant differences when compared to classical *Sharia'a*.

Saudi Arabia and some of the Gulf states do not have constitutions or legislatures. Their rulers have, to some extent, limited authority to change laws, given that they are based on *Sharia'a* as it is interpreted by their religious scholars. Iran shares some of these characteristics, but also has a parliament that legislates in a manner consistent with *Sharia'a*.

Although there are many different interpretations of *Sharia'a*, and differing perspectives on each interpretation, there is consensus among Muslims that *Sharia'a* is a reflection of God's will for mankind. *Sharia'a* must therefore be, in its purest sense, perfect and unchanging. The evolution or refinement of *Sharia'a* is an effort to reflect God's will more perfectly.

Trade and Banking

Islamic law recognises private and community property, as well as overlapping forms of entitlement for charitable purposes, known as *waqf* (trusts). Under *Sharia'a* law, however, ownership of all property ultimately rests with God. Although individual property rights are upheld, there is a corresponding obligation to share, particularly with those in need.

The laws of contract and obligation are also formed around this egalitarian *Qur'anic* requirement, prohibiting unequal exchanges or unfair advantage in trade. On this basis, the charging of interest on loans is prohibited, as are other transactions in which risks are borne disproportionately to the potential returns between parties to a transaction. The limits on personal liability afforded by incorporation are seen as a form of usury in this sense, as is conventional insurance.

All these inequities in risk and reward between parties to a transaction, known collectively as *riba*, are prohibited. For this reason, Islamic banking and financing arrangements are partnerships between customers and institutions, where risk and reward are distributed equitably. Partnerships, rather than corporations, are the key concept in collective Islamic business. Financing and investments are accomplished in this manner, with equity shifting over time between the institution and the client as payments are made or returns recognised.

The Islamic financial and investment models have taken root in the West and begun to flourish. Classic Islamic law details the manner of contracting, the types of transactions, the assignment of liability and reward, and the responsibilities of the parties in Islamic trade.

2.1.3 *Sharia'a* Supervisory Board

Islamic banks and banking institutions that offer Islamic banking products and services are required to establish a *Sharia'a* Supervisory Board (SSB) to advise them and to ensure that the operations and activities of the banking institutions comply with *Sharia'a* principles.

In Malaysia, the National *Sharia'a* Advisory Council, which has been set up at Bank Negara Malaysia (BNM), the central bank, advises BNM on the *Sharia'a* aspects of the operations of these institutions and on their products and services.

2.2   QUESTIONS

2.2.1   General

Circle true (T) or false (F) in the statements below. Note: you need to indicate T or F for each statement.

1. Under the *Sharia'a*, *riba* transactions are disliked but not explicitly prohibited in the *Qur'an*. **T   F**
2. One of the key questions that a *Sharia'a* Supervisory Board asks 'Is this the best investment for the *Rab ul Mall*?' **T   F**
3. One of the key questions that a *Sharia'a* Supervisory Board asks is 'As an asset manager is this a transaction in which a banker, as an individual, would be prepared to invest his own money?' **T   F**
4. A key *Sharia'a* principle, applied to Islamic banking, is that the good concerned in the transaction does not have to already exist. **T   F**
5. A key *Sharia'a* principle, applied to Islamic banking, is that money can be sold for money of more value than the original sum (*Bay-al-Mithl*). **T   F**
6. A key *Sharia'a* principle, applied to Islamic banking, is that any profits made in business transactions are *haram*. **T   F**
7. A key *Sharia'a* principle, applied to Islamic banking, is that a deferred sale at a lower price than the spot price is normal. **T   F**
8. A key *Sharia'a* principle, applied to Islamic banking, is that a deferred sale at a higher price than the spot price is normal. **T   F**
9. Models of Islamic banking are not mentioned in the *Qur'an* or in the *Hadith*, although the basic principles that govern the financial system are. **T   F**
10. The development of Islamic banking is based to a large degree on *Ijma*. **T   F**
11. *Ijma* is the direct and unmediated Word of Allah – the primary source of *Sharia'a* law. **T   F**

12. The sources of the *Sharia'a*, ranked in order of importance are as follows:
  • Holy *Qur'an*
  • *Qiyas*
  • *Hadith* and *Sunnah*
  • *Ijma*
  T F

13. The sources of the *Sharia'a*, ranked in order of importance are as follows:
  • Holy *Qur'an*
  • *Ijma*
  • *Qiyas*
  • *Hadith* and *Sunnah*
  T F

14. The sources of the *Sharia'a*, ranked in order of importance are as follows:
  • Holy *Qur'an*
  • *Hadith* and *Sunnah*
  • *Qiyas*
  • *Ijma*
  T F

15. The sources of the *Sharia'a*, ranked in order of importance are as follows:
  • Holy *Qur'an*
  • *Hadith* and *Sunnah*
  • *Ijma*
  • *Qiyas*
  T F

16. *Sunnah* means 'ancestral precedent' or 'custom of the tribe'.   **T   F**

17. *Qiyas* means the informed consensus of the community of scholars.   **T   F**

18. *Ijma* means the principle of using past analogies as precedent.   **T   F**

19. *Qiyas* means the principle of using past analogies as precedent.   **T   F**

20. *Sunnah* means the informed consensus of the community of scholars on the application of *Sharia'a* to worldly affairs.   **T   F**

21. *Ijma* means the informed consensus of the community of scholars on the application of *Sharia'a* to worldly affairs.   **T   F**

22. *Sharia'a* rules applied to Islamic banking are
  A. It is lawful to charge a higher price for a good than its current price if payments are to be made at a later date due to the fact that 'deferred payment' is *Sharia'a* compliant.   **T   F**
  B. The good concerned under *Sharia'a* rulings:
    i) must be in existence.
    ii) must be owned and possessed by the bank.
    iii) must have an instant and absolute sale.
    iv) must have a certain price with no conditions attached.
    If conditions (i–iv) above hold the *Fiqh* ruling is that a lending transaction and not a trading transaction are taking place.   **T   F**
  C. If conditions (i–iv) above hold the *Fiqh* ruling is that a trading transaction and not a lending transaction is taking place.   **T   F**

23. General *Sharia'a* rules applied to Islamic banking are
    A. Money cannot be sold for money of more value than the original sum (*Bay-al-Mithl*). **T   F**
    B. Any profits made are *haram*. **T   F**
    C. A deferred sale at a lower price than the spot price is usual. **T   F**
    D. A deferred sale at a higher price than the spot price is usual. **T   F**
24. The *Sharia'a* prohibits investing in companies associated with pork production because
    A. It is an act of obedience to the commands of Allah. **T   F**
    B. Pigs are deemed dirty animals and it is forbidden to eat the meat of an animal that feeds on dirt and filth. **T   F**
    C. Research shows there is a harmful effect on health of pork meat, lard (pork fat) and other pork by-products and any product that is harmful to people's health is deemed undesirable in Islam. **T   F**
    D. The *Qur'anic* injunction 'forbidden to you (for food) are: dead meat, blood, the flesh of swine and that on which hath been invoked the name of other than Allah'. **T   F**
25. The *Sharia'a* prohibits investing in companies associated with gambling because
    A. People can become very rich overnight and this is deemed unjust Islamically. **T   F**
    B. Islam promotes all that is pure and strives to exclude all impurities based on the principle that if something is entirely harmful it is *haram*, and if it is entirely beneficial it is *halal*. **T   F**
    C. It is a game of chance and does not necessarily promote a healthy attitude towards life with the effect that instead of investing energies into hard work and productive activities people can depend on, or daydream about, winning the lottery or in gambling. This behaviour can be counterproductive to the health of society. **T   F**
26. The *Sharia'a* prohibits investing in companies associated with tobacco because
    A. Islam prohibits buying, selling and usage of harmful substances. **T   F**
    B. Tobacco is highly addictive and extremely hazardous to health, not only of the smokers themselves but to those around them. **T   F**
    C. The *Hadith*, (teaching of prophet or his companions), states there should not be any infliction of harm to oneself or others. **T   F**
    D. It is proven that smoking of tobacco is very harmful given that tobacco is a cause of lung cancer. **T   F**
    E. Tobacco companies make vast profits, which is deemed an unIslamic concept. **T   F**

2.2.2   Responsibilities of the Parties to the *Sharia'a* Contracts

Circle true (T) or false (F) in the statements below. Note: you need to indicate T or F for each statement.

27. *Murabaha* is a type of leasing. **T   F**
28. *Salam* is a contract whereby the bank accepts an investment by the customer and invests the funds on the customer's behalf. **T   F**
29. *Ijara* is a contract whereby the bank buys the goods for the customer and sells them to the customer at a later date. **T   F**
30. *Istisna'a* is a contract whereby the bank accepts an investment by the customer and invests the funds on the customer's behalf. **T   F**

31. *Salam* is a purchase by a bank whereby the goods are delivered later but the payment is up front.   **T   F**
32. *Istisna'a* is a project whereby the bank and an investor both invest capital with both sharing the risks.   **T   F**
33. *Mudaraba* is a contract whereby the bank accepts an investment by the customer and invests the funds on the customer's behalf.   **T   F**
34. *Murabaha* is a project whereby the bank and an investor both invest capital with both sharing the risks.   **T   F**
35. *Istisna'a* is a contract whereby the bank buys the goods for the customer and sells them to the customer at a later date.   **T   F**
36. *Murabaha* is a contract whereby the bank buys the goods for the customer and then sells them to the customer at a later date.   **T   F**
37. *Salam* is a type of leasing.   **T   F**
38. *Murabaha* is an order by the bank to manufacture a specific physical capital asset for the purchaser.   **T   F**
39. *Istisna'a* is a purchase by a bank whereby the goods are delivered later but the payment is upfront.   **T   F**
40. *Murabaha* is a purchase by a bank whereby the goods are delivered later but the payment is upfront.   **T   F**
41. *Mudaraba* is a contract whereby the bank buys the goods for the customer and sells them to the customer at a later date.   **T   F**
42. *Musharaka* is a type of leasing.   **T   F**
43. *Istisna'a* is an order by the bank to manufacture a specific physical capital asset for the purchaser.   **T   F**
44. *Musharaka* is a contract whereby the bank accepts an investment by the customer and invests the funds on the customer's behalf.   **T   F**
45. *Mudaraba* is a project whereby the bank and an investor both invest capital with both sharing the risks.   **T   F**
46. *Ijara* is a type of leasing.   **T   F**
47. *Mudaraba* is a purchase by a bank whereby the goods are delivered later but the payment is upfront.   **T   F**
48. *Ijara* is a contract whereby the bank accepts an investment by the customer and invests the funds on the customer's behalf.   **T   F**
49. *Musharaka* is a project whereby the bank, and an investor, both invest capital with both sharing the risks.   **T   F**
50. *Mudaraba* is an order by the bank to manufacture a specific physical capital asset for the purchaser.   **T   F**
51. *Salam* is a project whereby the bank and an investor both invest capital with both sharing the risks.   **T   F**
52. *Ijara* is a project whereby the bank, and an investor, both invest capital with both sharing the risks.   **T   F**
53. *Musharaka* is a contract whereby the bank buys the goods for the customer and sells them to the customer at a later date.   **T   F**
54. *Ijara* is an order by the bank to manufacture a specific physical capital asset for the purchaser.   **T   F**
55. *Murabaha* is a contract whereby the bank accepts an investment by the customer and invests the funds on the customer's behalf.   **T   F**

56. *Ijara* is a purchase by a bank whereby the goods are delivered later but the payment is up front.   **T   F**
57. *Salam* is a contract whereby the bank buys the goods for the customer and sells them to the customer at a later date.   **T   F**
58. *Musharaka* is an order by the bank to manufacture a specific physical capital asset for the purchaser.   **T   F**
59. *Mudaraba* is a type of leasing.   **T   F**
60. *Musharaka* is a purchase by a bank whereby the goods are delivered later but the payment is upfront.   **T   F**
61. *Salam* is an order by the bank to manufacture a specific physical capital asset for the purchaser.   **T   F**
62. *Istisna'a* is a type of leasing.   **T   F**
63. *Musharaka* is a project whereby the bank and a partner both invest capital, with only the partner taking the risk of capital loss.   **T   F**
64. *Mudaraba* is a project whereby the bank and a partner both invest capital, with only the partner taking the risk of capital loss.   **T   F**
65. *Murabaha* is a project whereby the bank and a partner both invest capital, with only the partner taking the risk of capital loss.   **T   F**
66. *Ijara* is a project whereby the bank and a partner both invest capital, with only the partner taking the risk of capital loss.   **T   F**
67. *Istisna'a* is a project whereby the bank and a partner both invest capital, with only the partner taking the risk of capital loss.   **T   F**
68. *Salam* is a project whereby the bank and a partner both invest capital, with only the partner taking the risk of capital loss.   **T   F**
69. *Mudaraba* is a project whereby the bank invests capital and a partner provides managerial expertise, with only the bank taking the risk of capital loss.   **T   F**
70. *Musharaka* is a project whereby the bank invests capital and a partner provides managerial expertise, with only the bank taking the risk of capital loss.   **T   F**
71. *Murabaha* is a project whereby the bank invests capital and a partner provides managerial expertise, with only the bank taking the risk of capital loss.   **T   F**
72. *Istisna'a* is a project whereby the bank invests capital and a partner provides managerial expertise, with only the bank taking the risk of capital loss.   **T   F**
73. *Ijara* is a project whereby the bank invests capital and a partner provides managerial expertise, with only the bank taking the risk of capital loss.   **T   F**
74. *Salam* is a project whereby the bank invests capital and a partner provides managerial expertise, with only the bank taking the risk of capital loss.   **T   F**

2.2.3   Islamic Finance Terminology Quiz

Fill in the missing words indicated by the numbers in square brackets.

2.2.3.1   Ijara *Contract*

Ijara is a form of [75._____]. It involves a contract where the *Rab ul Mall* [76._____] and then leases an asset to a customer for a specified rental over a specific period. The duration of the lease, as well as the basis for rental, are agreed in advance. The bank retains [77._____] of the item throughout the arrangement and takes back the asset at the end of the contract.

2.2.3.2   Ijara wa Iqtina *Contract*

Ijara wa Iqtina is similar to *Ijara*, except that included in the contract is a [78._____] at a pre-agreed price. Rentals paid during the period of the lease constitute part of the purchase price. Often, as a result, the final sale will be for a token sum.

2.2.3.3   Musharaka *Contract*

Musharaka means partnership. It involves an investor placing his capital with an Islamic bank with both sharing the [79._____]. The difference between *Musharaka* contracts and *Mudaraba* contracts is that the partners can set any kind of [80._____] but losses in *Musharaka* must be [81._____] to the amount invested.

2.2.3.4   *Diminishing* Musharaka *Contract*

The principle of diminishing *Musharaka* can be used for home purchase. Diminishing *Musharaka* means that the bank [82._____] its equity in an asset with any additional capital payment the customer makes, over and above the [83._____]. The customer's ownership of the asset increases and the banks [84._____] by a similar amount each time the customer makes an additional capital payment. Ultimately, the bank transfers ownership of the asset entirely over to the customer.

2.2.3.5   Mudaraba *Contract*

Mudaraba refers to an investment on the customer's behalf by a bank. It takes the form of a contract between two parties, one who [85._____] and the other who [86._____] and who must agree to the division of any profits made in advance. In other words, the bank makes *Sharia'a*-compliant investments and shares the profits with the customer. If no profit is made, the financial loss is borne by the customer and the bank charges no fee.

2.2.3.6   Murabaha *Contract*

Murabaha is a contract for purchasing an asset and subsequent sale to the customer. This allows the customer to make purchases without having to take out a loan and [87._____]. The bank purchases the goods for the customer, and [88._____] them to the customer on a deferred basis, adding an [89._____]. The customer then pays the sale price for the goods on an instalment basis, effectively obtaining credit without paying interest.

2.2.3.7   Qard

The *Fiqh* definition of *Qard* is that it is a non-interest bearing loan intended to allow the borrower to use the loaned funds for a period of time with the understanding that [90._____].

2.2.3.8   Riba

Riba means interest, which is [91._____] in *Sharia'a* law. Any risk-free or guaranteed interest on a loan is considered to be [92._____].

2.3 ANSWERS

2.3.1 General

1. FALSE
2. FALSE
3. TRUE
4. FALSE
5. FALSE
6. FALSE
7. FALSE
8. TRUE
9. TRUE
10. TRUE
11. FALSE
12. FALSE
13. FALSE
14. FALSE
15. TRUE
16. TRUE
17. FALSE
18. FALSE
19. TRUE
20. FALSE
21. TRUE
22. A. TRUE
    B. FALSE
    C. TRUE
23. A. TRUE
    B. FALSE
    C. FALSE
    D. TRUE
24. A. TRUE
    B. TRUE
    C. TRUE
    D. TRUE
25. A. TRUE
    B. TRUE
    C. TRUE
26. A. TRUE
    B. TRUE
    C. TRUE
    D. TRUE
    E. FALSE

2.3.2   Responsibilities of the Parties to the *Sharia'a* Contracts

27. FALSE
28. FALSE
29. FALSE
30. FALSE
31. TRUE
32. FALSE
33. TRUE
34. FALSE
35. FALSE
36. TRUE
37. FALSE
38. FALSE
39. FALSE
40. FALSE
41. FALSE
42. FALSE
43. TRUE
44. FALSE
45. FALSE
46. TRUE
47. FALSE
48. FALSE
49. TRUE
50. FALSE
51. FALSE
52. FALSE
53. FALSE
54. FALSE
55. FALSE
56. FALSE
57. FALSE
58. FALSE
59. FALSE
60. FALSE
61. FALSE
62. FALSE
63. FALSE
64. FALSE
65. FALSE
66. FALSE
67. FALSE
68. FALSE
69. TRUE
70. FALSE
71. FALSE

72. FALSE
73. FALSE
74. FALSE

2.3.3   Islamic Finance Terminology Quiz

75. Leasing
76. Buys
77. Ownership
78. Promise from the customer to buy the asset at the end of the lease period
79. Risk and return
80. Profit-sharing ratio
81. Proportionate
82. Reduces
83. Rental payments
84. Decreases
85. Provides the funds
86. Provides the expertise
87. Pay interest
88. Sells
89. Agreed profit margin
90. It is redeemed in due course
91. Prohibited
92. Not *Sharia'a* compliant (*haram*)

3

Principles of Islamic Banking
and Finance

3.1 LEARNING OUTCOMES, SUMMARY OVERVIEW AND PROBLEMS

3.1.1 Learning Outcomes

After reading Chapter 3 you should be able to do the following:

- Describe the key principles underlying Islamic banking.
- Contrast conventional banking with Islamic banking.
- Explain profit and loss sharing principles.
- Define the variants of *riba*.
- Explain the Islamic rationale for the ban on *riba*.
- Describe *riba* in the *Qur'an*.
- Identify issues involving asymmetric information.
- Describe *riba* in the *Sunnah*.
- Explain risk sharing.
- Identify the textual evidence for the ban on *riba*.
- Explain the concept of *gharar*.
- Explain the concept of 'making money out of money'.
- Test that you have fully understood the principles that drive Islamic banking and finance.

3.1.2 Summary Overview

Islamic banking refers to a system of banking activity that is consistent with the principles of Islamic law (*Sharia'a*) and its practical application through the development of Islamic economics. *Sharia'a* prohibits the payment or acceptance of interest for the lending and accepting of money respectively (*riba*, usury) for specific terms, as well as investing in businesses that provide goods or services considered contrary to its principles (*haram*, forbidden).

Although these principles were used as the basis for a flourishing economy in earlier times, only in the late 20th century were a number of Islamic banks formed to apply these principles to private or semi-private commercial institutions.

3.1.2.1 Riba

The word '*riba*' means excess, increase or addition, which according to *Sharia'a* terminology, implies any excess compensation without due consideration. Consideration does not include the time value of money. The definition of riba in classical Islamic jurisprudence was 'surplus value without counterpart'.

3.1.3   History of Islamic Banking

During the Islamic Golden Age, early forms of proto-capitalism and free markets were present in the Caliphate, where an early market economy and an early form of mercantilism were developed between the 8th–12th centuries, which some refer to as 'Islamic capitalism'.

A number of economic concepts and techniques were applied in early Islamic banking, including bills of exchange, the first forms of partnership (*Mufawada*), limited partnerships (*Mudaraba*), and the earliest forms of capital (*al-mal*), capital accumulation (*nama al-mal*), cheques, promissory notes, trusts (*waqf*), transactional accounts, ledgers and assignments.

Business enterprises, independent from the state, also existed in the medieval Islamic world, and the institution of 'agency' was also introduced during that time. Many of these early capitalist concepts were adopted and further advanced in medieval Europe from the 13th century onwards.

3.1.3.1   Modern Islamic Banking

Interest-free banking is of very recent origin. The earliest references to the reorganisation of banking on the basis of profit sharing rather than interest are found in academic work done in the 1940s and 1950s.

This work, which perceived the 'necessary evil' allowability of commercial banks, proposed a banking system based on the concept of *Mudaraba*: profit and loss sharing.

Over the next two decades, interest-free banking attracted more attention, partly because of the political interest it created in Pakistan and partly because of the emergence of young Muslim economists. Academic works specifically devoted to this subject began to appear in this period.

The early 1970s saw institutional involvement. The Conference of the Finance Ministers of the Islamic Countries held in Karachi in 1970, the Egyptian study in 1972, the First International Conference on Islamic Economics in Mecca in 1976 and the International Economic Conference in London in 1977 were the result of such involvement. The involvement of institutions and governments led to the application of theory to practice and resulted in the establishment of the first interest-free banks.

The Islamic Development Bank, an inter-governmental bank established in 1975, was born of this process.

The first modern experiment with Islamic banking was undertaken in Egypt without projecting an Islamic image – for fear of being seen as a manifestation of Islamic fundamentalism (anathema to the political regime). The pioneering effort, led by Ahmad El Naggar, took the form of a savings bank based on profit-sharing in the Egyptian town of Mit Ghamr in 1963. This experiment lasted until 1967.

In 1972, the Mit Ghamr Savings project became part of Nasr Social Bank which, currently, is still in business in Egypt. The first modern commercial Islamic bank, Dubai Islamic Bank, opened its doors in 1975. In the early years, the products offered were basic and strongly founded on conventional banking products, but in recent years the industry has poineered its own Islamic Model.

3.1.4   Islamic Banking Principles

Islamic banking has the same purpose as conventional banking except that it operates in accordance with the rules of *Sharia'a*, known as *Fiqh al-Muamalat* (Islamic rules on transactions). The basic principle of Islamic banking is the sharing of profit and loss and the prohibition of riba (usury). Common terms used in Islamic banking include profit sharing (*Mudaraba*), safekeeping (*Wadiah*), joint venture (*Musharaka*), cost plus (Murabaha) and leasing (*Ijara*).

In an Islamic mortgage transaction, instead of loaning the buyer money to purchase the item, a bank might buy the item itself from the seller, and re-sell it to the buyer at a profit, while allowing the buyer to pay the bank in instalments. In order to protect itself against default, the bank asks for collateral. The goods or land is registered to the name of the buyer from the start of the transaction. This arrangement is called *Murabaha*.

An innovative approach applied by some banks for home loans, called *Diminishing Musharaka,* allows for a floating rate in the form of rental. The bank and borrower form a partnership entity, both providing capital at an agreed percentage to purchase the property. The partnership entity then rents out the property to the borrower and charges rent. The bank and the borrower then share the proceeds from this rent based on the current equity share of the partnership.

At the same time, the borrower in the partnership entity also buys the bank's share of the property at agreed instalments until the full equity is transferred to the borrower and the partnership is ended. If default occurs, both the bank and the borrower receive a proportion of the proceeds from the sale of the property based on each party's current equity.

Mudaraba is venture capital funding of an entrepreneur who provides labour while financing is provided by the bank so that both profit and risk are shared. Such participatory arrangements between capital and labour reflect the Islamic view that the borrower must not bear all the risk/cost of a failure, resulting in a balanced distribution of income.

Islamic banking is restricted to Islamically acceptable transactions, which exclude those involving alcohol, pork, gambling and so on. The aim of this is to engage in only ethical investing, and moral purchasing.

Islamic banks have grown recently in the Muslim world but remain a very small share of the global banking system.

3.2 QUESTIONS

3.2.1 General

Circle true (T) or false (F) in the statements below. Note: you need to indicate T or F for each statement.

1. The main objectives of Islamic banks are to:
   A. Make attractive returns for the shareholders.   **T   F**
   B. Ensure that *haram* activities are not financed.   **T   F**
   C. Provide an alternative to interest-based finance.   **T   F**
   D. Finance the building of mosques.   **T   F**
2. The principles of an economy based on Islam are to:
   A. Ensure the realisation of socio-economic justice.   **T   F**
   B. Establish harmony between the moral and the material needs of society.   **T   F**
   C. Properly utilise and distribute scarce resources given by Allah to mankind.   **T   F**
   D. Provide freely available financing for Muslims with good investment ideas.   **T   F**

3. Applying Islamic banking principles:
   A. The *Rab ul Mall* has no right to an automatic reward for supplying finance unless he shares in the provision of entrepreneurial skills.   **T   F**
   B. The creditor/debtor relationship does not apply.   **T   F**
   C. Borrowers would not need to pay interest on their loans.   **T   F**
   D. The *Rab ul Mall* becomes a partner in the business or project, sharing in the provision of entrepreneurial skills.   **T   F**

4. The Islamic financial system is grounded on the following basic principles:
   A. Risk sharing – the terms of financial transactions need to reflect a symmetric risk/return distribution that each participant to the transaction may face.   **T   F**
   B. Materiality – a financial transaction needs to have a material effect, which is directly or indirectly linked to a real economic transaction.   **T   F**
   C. No exploitation – a financial transaction should not lead to the exploitation of any party to the transaction.   **T   F**
   D. No financing of sinful activities such as the production of alcoholic beverages.   **T   F**
   E. Shareholder returns are not a criteria for judging success.   **T   F**

5. The following are some characteristics of conventional banks:
   A. Assets are long term while liabilities are short term.   **T   F**
   B. Asset/liability mismatches have adequate hedging solutions.   **T   F**
   C. Religious factors are applied to asset management.   **T   F**
   D. Money is lent to wherever good returns are available.   **T   F**

6. The following are some characteristics of Islamic banks:
   A. Assets are long term while liabilities are short term.   **T   F**
   B. Asset/liability mismatches do not have adequate *Sharia'a* compliant hedging solutions.   **T   F**
   C. Religious factors are applied to asset management.   **T   F**
   D. Money is lent to wherever good returns are available.   **T   F**

7. Applying Islamic financial principles means that:
   A. Islamic financial institutions are not allowed to extend lines of credit that bear interest receivables.   **T   F**
   B. Banks have to make money out of money.   **T   F**
   C. Profit sharing is the only alternative to *riba*.   **T   F**
   D. Deferred sale contracts are one of the favoured modes of finance.   **T   F**

8. The following are Islamically acceptable modes of finance:
   A. *Murabaha* – the object of sale is delivered at the contract time and the price becomes due as a debt.   **T   F**
   B. *Salam* sale – the price is paid at the time of contract and the object of sale becomes due as a debt in kind.   **T   F**
   C. *Salam* sale – the price is paid at the time the object of sale is delivered.   **T   F**
   D. *Istisna'a* – the price is paid at the time of contract and the object of sale is to be manufactured and delivered later.   **T   F**
   E. *Ijara* – the sale of the use of rights on assets where assets are delivered to the user, who in turn pays periodical rentals.   **T   F**

9. Applying Islamic finance principles results in:
   A. Interest *(riba)* being prohibited – the central tenet of the Islamic financial system.   **T   F**
   B. The *Rab ul Mall* becomes a creditor instead of an investor.   **T   F**

C. The *Rab ul Mall* and the entrepreneur share business risks in return for a share of the profits.   **T   F**

D. The *Rab ul Mall* becomes an investor instead of a creditor.   **T   F**

10. The principles of Islamic finance include:

A. Prohibition of speculative behaviour.   **T   F**

B. Sanctity of contracts.   **T   F**

C. Only *Sharia'a*-approved activities permissible.   **T   F**

D. Lending surplus funds to other Islamic banks.   **T   F**

11. Islamic banking involves:

A. Bank management by *Sharia'a* scholars.   **T   F**

B. Prohibition of usury, gambling and *gharar.*   **T   F**

C. Avoiding risky investing.   **T   F**

12. Conventional banks:

A. Pay interest to borrowers.   **T   F**

B. Charge interest to depositors.   **T   F**

C. Base their lending criteria largely on collateral.   **T   F**

D. Can apply standard asset/liability procedures.   **T   F**

13. Islamic banks:

A. Pay interest to borrowers.   **T   F**

B. Accept interest on their liabilities but donate it to charity.   **T   F**

C. Base their investing criteria on the investment potential and not just on collateral.   **T   F**

D. Can apply standard asset/liability procedures.   **T   F**

14. Islamic banks have a predominance of:

A. Liquid assets.   **T   F**

B. Illiquid assets.   **T   F**

C. Liquid liabilities.   **T   F**

D. Illiquid liabilities.   **T   F**

15. Conventional banks have a predominance of:

A. Liquid assets.   **T   F**

B. Illiquid assets.   **T   F**

C. Liquid liabilities.   **T   F**

D. Illiquid liabilities.   **T   F**

16. Every loan made by a conventional bank is a contract between the bank and the client with the following essential features:

A. A creditor/borrower relationship is established.   **T   F**

B. The borrower has a time limit specifying specific date(s) on which a certain percentage of interest, on borrowed capital, becomes due for payment, along with the principal.   **T   F**

C. The income of the bank is known and prefixed and is not in any way related to the income or profits of the borrower.   **T   F**

D. Interest income is donated to charity.   **T   F**

17. The features of Islamic banking are as follows:

A. It is a contract between two partners – the *Rab ul Mall* and the client – providing a partner/partner relationship.   **T   F**

B. The contract has a time limit in the sense that the client has to return the capital on/within specific date(s) or contingent on certain outcomes. However, the return to the bank is not fixed either from the standpoint of time or to that of the rate paid.   **T   F**

C. The *Rab ul Mall* shares a prefixed ratio of profit expressed in percentage terms. This is not a prefixed rate of return calculated on capital advanced. Thus, income (profit) for the bank, unlike the practice of its conventional counterpart, fluctuates with the profits of the borrower.   **T   F**

D. Collateral, posted with some *Sharia'a* contracts, ensures that the *Rab ul Mall* faces limited default risk.   **T   F**

18. The Arabic term *riba* means:
    A. Any increment over the principal invested.   **T   F**
    B. Any increment over the principal lent out.   **T   F**
    C. 'Those who devour *riba* will not stand except as stands one whom the Evil by his touch has driven to madness'.   **T   F**
    D. Profit and loss sharing.   **T   F**
    E. *Murabaha.*   **T   F**

19. The following can be considered as characteristics that distinguish Islamic banks from conventional banks:
    A. Complete elimination of the factor of usury (interest) from all financial dealings.   **T   F**
    B. Accountability to the *Sharia'a* Supervisory Board to ensure that its operations and assets are free of the interest element.   **T   F**
    C. Acting as universal multi-purpose institutions embodying the functions of both commercial and investment banks.   **T   F**
    D. Directing the use of funds in a manner that contributes primarily to the generation of economic activity designed to give rise to socio-economic justice within society.   **T   F**
    E. Applying religious beliefs given that their shareholders are not interested in high returns.   **T   F**

20. Islamic banks:
    A. Provide competitive returns to their depositors.   **T   F**
    B. Work closely with providers of funds (depositors) in the use of their funds.   **T   F**
    C. Use a high level of expertise and technical know-how for careful evaluation of financing and investment proposals and maintain close monitoring to ensure profitable use of the funds provided.   **T   F**
    D. Enhance the research and development process in order to develop new products within the precepts of Islamic *Sharia'a.*   **T   F**

21. The definitions of the key components of the *Sharia'a* are:
    A. *Sunnah* – meaning 'ancestral precedent' or 'custom of the tribe'.   **T   F**
    B. *Sunnah* – meaning practice and precept of the prophet Mohammed as transmitted by the narrators of authentic tradition (*Hadith*).   **T   F**
    C. *Ijma* – meaning informed consensus of the community of scholars on the application of *Sharia'a* to worldly affairs.   **T   F**
    D. *Qiyas* – meaning the principle of using past analogies as precedent.   **T   F**

22. The investment implications of not allowing *riba* are prohibitions on:
    A. Investing in interest bearing debt.   **T   F**
    B. Receiving interest or other un-pure income.   **T   F**

    C. Trading in debts at a price other than at their face value.   **T   F**

    D. Home financing mortgages.   **T   F**

23. Applying profit and loss sharing principles in Islamic banking should result in:

    A. Justice and fairness to all concerned.   **T   F**

    B. Entrepreneurs being penalised by obliging them to return the principal even when part of it is lost due to circumstances beyond the entrepreneur's control.   **T   F**

    C. Economic justice given that it requires that capital seeking profit shares the risk attached to profit making.   **T   F**

    D. The payment obligations of the entrepreneur being fixed in amount.   **T   F**

24. Applying profit and loss sharing principles by Islamic banks results in:

    A. Investing funds on the basis of the expected productivity of projects rather than on the criterion of the creditworthiness of those who borrow money.   **T   F**

    B. More projects being considered on their merit rather than the creditworthiness of the borrowers.   **T   F**

    C. Innovative creditworthy entrepreneurs preferring debt finance.   **T   F**

25. Some of the key questions that a *Sharia'a* Supervisory Board asks are:

    A. Do the terms of the transaction comply with *Sharia'a* law?   **T   F**

    B. Is this the best investment for the bank?   **T   F**

    C. Does the investment produce value for the client and for the community or society in which the client is active?   **T   F**

    D. As an asset manager, is this a transaction in which a banker, as an individual, would be prepared to invest his own money?   **T   F**

26. The characteristics of Islamic banking are:

    A. Transactions must be based on tangible assets and not intangible assets.   **T   F**

    B. Islamic banking contracts should be clear and free from *jahala* (ignorance); *gharar* (uncertainty in the contractual obligation); debt trading and short selling.   **T   F**

    C. Deferred contracts are permissible.   **T   F**

    D. Relationships between banks and suppliers/users of capital must be based on sharing of profits/losses.   **T   F**

27. When referring to *riba* transactions in the *Qur'an*:

    A. Transactions are explicitly prohibited in the *Qur'an*.   **T   F**

    B. Investors must be compensated by other means than *riba*.   **T   F**

    C. The disregard of the prohibition of interest puts one at war with God and his prophet Mohammed.   **T   F**

    D. Punishments on earth for accepting *riba* are clearly set out.   **T   F**

    E. Temporal punishment for an unrepentant perpetrator is not prescribed.   **T   F**

28. *Riba* occurs in the following contract.

    A power station is drawing up a contract between itself and a large consumer of electricity (the off taker). The contract provides that if the off taker breaches its obligations under the contract, the producer has the right to terminate the contract and transfer the generation facility (built by the producer) to the off taker for the 'purchase price'. The purchase price is to be calculated in accordance with the following formula:

- the amount spent by the producer in construction of the facility plus
- the amount of such funds compounded annually at 15% for each year of the contract before termination.

T   F

29. Penalty clauses in Islamic financing projects:
    A. Are forbidden because they are an imposed increase (*riba*) in the liability of one of the parties.   **T   F**
    B. Are the only way to ensure the project is finished on time.   **T   F**
    C. Should be resolved in the law courts.   **T   F**
    D. Must be resolved by the *Sharia'a* Supervisory Board.   **T   F**

30. What are the problems with *Sharia'a* Supervisory Boards deciding on *Fatawa*?
    A. The diversity of views held by Muslim scholars.   **T   F**
    B. *Fatawa* are sometimes given by *Sharia'a* scholars from the same financial institution they are working for, leading to a conflict of interest potential.   **T   F**
    C. There is a dearth of scholars well versed in both The *Qur'an* and economics, finance and capital markets.   **T   F**
    D. *Sharia'a* scholars are only concerned with the strict application of the *Qur'an*.   **T   F**

31. The main objectives of Islamic banks include:
    A. Stewardship, mobilising surplus funds, attracting them by providing *halal* (free of interest) yet competitive investment returns.   **T   F**
    B. Channelling of funds essentially to trade or production-related activities in order that economic activities are enhanced.   **T   F**
    C. Marketing Islamic banking principally to Muslims.   **T   F**
    D. Providing financial support on an ethical basis ensuring that investments do not contribute to undue concentration of wealth in a few hands but rather support value creation by offering the required level of technological expertise and management know-how.   **T   F**
    E. Providing banking services to clients efficiently, helping them to undertake their financial dealings in conformity with the *Sharia'a*.   **T   F**

32. Islamic Banks act as Trustees with the effect that:
    A. Unlike traditional banks, whose client deposits they accept, Islamic banks are purely intermediaries, carrying out trust and advisory functions.   **T   F**
    B. Client funds (except for demand deposits) are all fiduciary.   **T   F**
    C. Islamic banks maintain a greater balance between the interests of the depositors, shareholders, the users of funds and society, whereas traditional banks exploit market imperfections to obtain maximum results for the benefit of their shareholders.   **T   F**
    D. Islamic banks risk suffering larger losses than conventional banks.   **T   F**

33. Due to the nature of Islamic banks, and their contractual relationship with their depositors, it is argued they are relatively less risky than conventional banks for a number of reasons:
    A. For an Islamic bank, deposits other than demand deposits do not count as bank liabilities with the effect that Islamic banks are therefore deemed less highly leveraged institutions than traditional banks.   **T   F**
    B. Concepts such as financial returns do not have the same significance as in the case of conventional banks, because an Islamic bank does not guarantee repayment of profit and capital.   **T   F**
    C. Bank management does not believe in undertaking risky transactions.   **T   F**
    D. Depositors with an Islamic bank are deeply involved in its operations with the effect that Islamic banks are less likely to experience a run on deposits in the event of an economic upheaval or drastic change in market conditions.   **T   F**
    E. Debt to equity and debt to assets ratios are not so relevant because financing is made in the form of prepayments and not direct lending.   **T   F**

3.2.2   Islamic Banking Principles

34. One of the main objectives of Islamic banks is to ensure that *halal* activities are not financed.   **T   F**
35. One of the main objectives of Islamic banks is to provide an alternative to conventional debt-based finance.   **T   F**
36. The principles of an economy, based on Islam, are to provide freely available financing for sound Islamic investments.   **T   F**
37. When applying Islamic banking principles the creditor/debtor relationship breaks down.   **T   F**
38. When applying Islamic banking principles the borrower would still need to pay interest on their loans.   **T   F**
39. One of the basic principles of the Islamic financial system is that shareholder returns are not a criteria for judging success.   **T   F**
40. One of the effects of applying Islamic banking principles is that assets become long term whilst liabilities remain short term.   **T   F**
41. One of the effects of applying Islamic banking principles is that asset/liability mismatches cannot occur.   **T   F**
42. One of the effects of applying Islamic banking principles is that money is lent to wherever good returns are available.   **T   F**
43. Applying Islamic financial principles means that Islamic financial institutions are allowed to accept collateral which involves interest payables but not interest receivables.   **T   F**
44. Applying Islamic financial principles means that the *Rab ul Mall* has to make money out of money.   **T   F**
45. Applying Islamic financial principles means that profit sharing is the only alternative to *riba*.   **T   F**
46. Applying Islamic financial principles means that deferred sale contracts are one of the favoured modes of finance.   **T   F**
47. Applying Islamic financial principles results in the *Rab ul Mall* becoming a creditor instead of an investor.   **T   F**
48. Applying Islamic financial principles results in the *Rab ul Mall* becoming an investor instead of a creditor.   **T   F**
49. One of the effects of applying the principles of Islamic finance is the prohibition of conventional derivatives.   **T   F**
50. Islamic banking practice results in the *Sharia'a* being the central regulatory authority.   **T   F**
51. Islamic banking involves the acceptability of usury.   **T   F**
52. Islamic banking involves avoiding risky investing.   **T   F**
53. The *Rab ul Mall* pays interest to borrowers.   **T   F**
54. The *Rab ul Mall* base their investing criteria on profit and loss share principles and do not use collateral.   **T   F**
55. The income (profit) for the *Rab ul Mall*, unlike the practice of its conventional counterpart, fluctuates with the profits of the lender.   **T   F**
56. *Riba* means profit and loss sharing.   **T   F**
57. *Riba* means an increment over capital.   **T   F**
58. One of the investment implications of not allowing *riba* are prohibitions on receiving interest or other un-pure income.   **T   F**

59. One of the investment implications of not allowing *riba* are prohibitions on trading in debts at a price other than at their face value.   **T   F**
60. Applying profit and loss sharing principles, in Islamic banking, results in the payment obligations of the entrepreneur being fixed in amount.   **T   F**
61. Applying profit and loss sharing principles, in Islamic banking, results in innovative creditworthy entrepreneurs preferring debt finance.   **T   F**
62. One of the effects of applying the principles of Islamic finance is that transactions must be based on intangible assets.   **T   F**
63. One of the characteristics of Islamic banking is that Islamic banking contracts should not depend on *Ijtihad*.   **T   F**
64. One of the characteristics of Islamic banking is that Islamic banking contracts should not depend on *Istisna'a*.   **T   F**
65. One of the characteristics of Islamic banking is that Islamic banking contracts should be free from *gharar*.   **T   F**
66. One of the effects of applying the principles of Islamic finance is that deferred contracts are impermissible.   **T   F**
67. One of the effects of applying the principles of Islamic finance is that the relationship between the *Rab ul Mall* and the borrowers is that the deal must be based on the sharing of profits but not of losses.   **T   F**
68. Penalty clauses in Islamic financing projects are the only *halal* way to ensure that the project is finished on time.   **T   F**
69. Penalty clauses in Islamic financing projects are *haram* because they are an imposed increase in the liability of one of the parties.   **T   F**
70. Disputes concerning penalty clauses in Islamic banking projects should be resolved by the Law Courts and not by the *Sharia'a* Supervisory Board.   **T   F**

3.3   ANSWERS

3.3.1   General

1. A. FALSE
   B. TRUE
   C. TRUE
   D. FALSE
2. A. TRUE
   B. TRUE
   C. TRUE
   D. FALSE
3. A. TRUE
   B. TRUE
   C. TRUE
   D. TRUE
4. A. TRUE
   B. TRUE
   C. TRUE
   D. TRUE
   E. FALSE

5. A. TRUE
    B. TRUE
    C. FALSE
    D. FALSE
6. A. TRUE
    B. FALSE
    C. TRUE
    D. FALSE
7. A. TRUE
    B. FALSE
    C. FALSE
    D. TRUE
8. A. TRUE
    B. TRUE
    C. FALSE
    D. TRUE
    E. TRUE
9. A. TRUE
    B. FALSE
    C. TRUE
    D. TRUE
10. A. TRUE
    B. TRUE
    C. TRUE
    D. FALSE
11. A. FALSE
    B. TRUE
    C. FALSE
12. A. FALSE
    B. FALSE
    C. TRUE
    D. TRUE
13. A. FALSE
    B. FALSE
    C. TRUE
    D. FALSE
14. A. FALSE
    B. TRUE
    C. TRUE
    D. FALSE
15. A. TRUE
    B. FALSE
    C. FALSE
    D. FALSE
16. A. TRUE
    B. TRUE

   C. TRUE
   D. FALSE
17. A. TRUE
   B. TRUE
   C. TRUE
   D. TRUE
18. A. FALSE
   B. TRUE
   C. FALSE
   D. FALSE
   E. FALSE
19. A. TRUE
   B. TRUE
   C. TRUE
   D. TRUE
   E. FALSE
20. A. FALSE
   B. TRUE
   C. TRUE
   D. TRUE
21. A. TRUE
   B. TRUE
   C. TRUE
   D. TRUE
22. A. TRUE
   B. TRUE
   C. TRUE
   D. FALSE
23. A. TRUE
   B. FALSE
   C. TRUE
   D. FALSE
24. A. TRUE
   B. TRUE
   C. TRUE
25. A. TRUE
   B. FALSE
   C. TRUE
   D. TRUE
26. A. FALSE
   B. TRUE
   C. TRUE
   D. TRUE
27. A. TRUE
   B. TRUE
   C. TRUE
   D. FALSE
   E. TRUE

28. TRUE
29. A. TRUE
    B. FALSE
    C. TRUE
    D. FALSE
30. A. TRUE
    B. TRUE
    C. TRUE
    D. FALSE
31. A. TRUE
    B. TRUE
    C. FALSE
    D. TRUE
    E. TRUE
32. A. TRUE
    B. TRUE
    C. TRUE
    D. TRUE
33. A. TRUE
    B. TRUE
    C. FALSE
    D. FALSE
    E. TRUE
34. A. TRUE
    B. FALSE
    C. TRUE
35. TRUE
36. FALSE
37. TRUE
38. FALSE
39. FALSE
40. TRUE
41. FALSE
42. FALSE
43. FALSE
44. TRUE
45. FALSE
46. TRUE
47. FALSE
48. TRUE
49. TRUE
50. FALSE
51. FALSE
52. FALSE
53. FALSE
54. FALSE
55. TRUE
56. FALSE

57. TRUE
58. TRUE
59. TRUE
60. FALSE
61. TRUE
62. FALSE
63. FALSE
64. TRUE
65. TRUE
66. FALSE
67. FALSE
68. FALSE
69. TRUE
70. TRUE

4

The *Murabaha* Contract as a Mode of Islamic Finance

4.1 LEARNING OUTCOMES, SUMMARY OVERVIEW AND PROBLEMS

4.1.1 Learning Outcomes

After reading Chapter 4 you should be able to do the following:

- Define *Murabaha*.
- Explain the treatment of money within Islam.
- Distinguish a conventional loan from a *Murabaha* contract.
- Describe the elements of a *Murabaha* transaction.
- Contrast *Murabaha* with the other modes of Islamic finance.
- Identify the reasoning behind the *Sharia'a* rulings on *Murabaha*.
- Explain the practicalities of implementing *Murabaha*.
- Identify the Arabic terminology used in *Murabaha*.
- Explain the role that interest can play within a *Murabaha* transaction.
- Explain the importance of deferred sales within Islamic finance.
- Describe the *Sharia'a* rulings on *Murabaha*.
- Contrast the role of penalty defaults within conventional and Islamic finance.
- Define *Musawama*.
- Identify problems with applying *Murabaha*.
- Explain how *Murabaha* can be used for home finance.
- Define LIBOR and explain its application with a *Murabaha* contract.
- Identify the deferred sale versus profit and loss share (PLS) contracts.
- Test that you have fully understood the principles that underlie the *Murabaha* contract.

4.1.2 Summary Overview

Murabaha is a particular kind of sale, compliant with Sharia'a, where the seller expressly identifies the cost he has incurred for the commodities for sale and sells it to another person by adding some profit or mark-up thereon which is known to the buyer.

Murabaha is one of the most popular modes used by Islamic banks to promote *riba*-free transactions.

4.1.2.1 What Does Murabaha Mean?

Murabaha is an Islamic financing structure, where an intermediary buys an asset with free and clear title to it. The intermediary and prospective buyer then agree upon a sale price (including an agreed upon profit for the intermediary) that can be made through a series of instalments, or as a lump sum payment.

Murabaha is not an interest-bearing loan, which would be considered *riba* (or excess), but is an acceptable form of credit sale under *Sharia'a* (Islamic religious law).

It is important to note that to prevent *riba*, the intermediary cannot be compensated in addition to the agreed upon terms of the contract. For this reason, if the buyer is late in his payments, the intermediary cannot charge any late penalties.

There are practical guidelines in place to help ensure that the *Murabaha* transaction between a bank and a customer is one based on trade and not merely a financing transaction. For instance, the bank must take constructive or actual possession of the good before selling it to the customer. The bank can only impose penalties for late payment by agreeing to 'purify' them by donating them to charity.

Murabaha is often referred to as 'cost-plus financing' and frequently appears as a form of trade finance based upon letters of credit. In its simplest form, this contract involves the sale of an item on a deferred basis.

The item is delivered immediately and the price to be paid for the item includes a mutually agreed margin of profit payable to the seller. In this contract, the market cost price (true cost) of the item is shared with the buyer at the time of concluding the sale.

Murabaha is a form of 'trust sale' because the buyer must trust that the seller is disclosing his true costs. After discussing the true costs, a profit margin may be agreed either on a percentage of cost basis or as a fixed amount. It is very important to remember that the amount of profit earned in this transaction is not a reward for the use of the financier's money. In other words, a financier cannot take money if he does not perform any service other than the use of his money for the transaction. Such an occurrence would cause this type of deal to resemble the charging of interest.

Today, *Murabaha* is used most to assist short-term trade transactions.

To help clarify the process, *Murabaha* is depicted as a flow chart in Figure 4.1. The *Murabaha* financing mode comprises more than 75% of Islamic banks' financing activities. Although Islam encourages PLS-based solutions, these account for only 10% or so. The PLS principle is rarely strictly applied.

Since Islamic banks, appear to survive primarily on non-PLS financing techniques, this has been referred to as a legal embarrassment for purists in the Islamic finance industry. That so many banks and clients prefer the *Murabaha* method of financing is, however, not particularly surprising.

The bank is taking larger risks, and must often cope with excessive project evaluation costs when using the PLS-financing methods. At the same time, because the amount owed to the bank in a profit-sharing contract often exceeds the amount to be paid in a *Murabaha* contract, the borrowers also face potentially higher borrowing costs in PLS-mode financing, when the project succeeds.

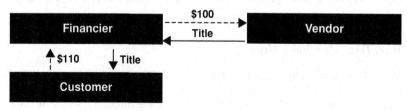

Figure 4.1 *Murabaha* – cost-plus financing

Accordingly, banks and borrowers often choose the *Murabaha* mark-up mode. This development is often referred to as the '*Murabaha* syndrome'.

Another concern is that Islamic banks have significantly twisted the principle of *Murabaha*. They have, on occasions, on Islamically-dubious grounds, justified *Sharia'a*-non compliant behaviour: for example, the allowance of the time-value of money concept and the enforcement of penalty fees on clients who are unable to pay.

4.2 QUESTIONS

4.2.1 What are the Features of the *Murabaha* Contract?

1. How does it work?

   _____

   _____

   _____

   _____

2. In what sense is *Murabaha* an asset-based or equity-based source of finance?

   _____

   _____

   _____

   _____

3. What is the risk for the *Rab ul Mall* providing *Murabaha* finance?

   _____

   _____

   _____

   _____

4.2.2 The *Murabaha* Contract

Circle true (T) or false (F) in the statements below. Note: you need to indicate T or F for each statement.

4. *Murabaha* is an Arabic term that means
   A. A deferred credit sale.   **T   F**
   B. A sale with a mutually agreed profit for the *Rab ul Mall*.   **T   F**
   C. The *Rab ul Mall* acts as a middle man.   **T   F**
5. Which of the following are features of a *Murabaha*:
   A. The seller discloses the cost price to the *Rab ul Mall*.   **T   F**
   B. An undisclosed profit rate is added by the *Rab ul Mall*.   **T   F**
   C. The *Rab ul Mall* owns the product before selling it.   **T   F**

6. Which of the following is a *Sharia'a* ruling for a valid sale:
    A. The existence of the asset.   **T   F**
    B. The sale price to be specified later.   **T   F**
    C. A valid sale contract exists.   **T   F**
7. The *Murabaha* asset, after being bought, is initially owned by:
    A. The *Rab ul Mall*.   **T   F**
    B. The client.   **T   F**
    C. The manufacturer.   **T   F**
8. If there is default by the buyer:
    A. The *Rab ul Mall* can renegotiate the price.   **T   F**
    B. The *Rab ul Mall* can charge late payment fees.   **T   F**
    C. The buyer must donate money to charity.   **T   F**
9. A key feature of the *Murabaha* transaction is that:
    A. Money is being sold for money.   **T   F**
    B. A commodity is being sold for money.   **T   F**
    C. A commodity is being sold for a commodity.   **T   F**
10. With *Murabaha*:
    A. No roll-over is permitted.   **T   F**
    B. No price renegotiation is permitted.   **T   F**
    C. The price to the buyer is fixed.   **T   F**
    D. No late penalty, payable to the *Rab ul Mall*, is permitted.   **T   F**
11. The following forms of collateral are accepted with *Murabaha*:
    A. The asset purchased.   **T   F**
    B. Any other property.   **T   F**
    C. Third party guarantees.   **T   F**
    D. A personal guarantee.   **T   F**
12. The elements that make *Murabaha Sharia'a* compliant are:
    A. The *Rab ul Mall* is selling goods for money on a deferred basis.   **T   F**
    B. Money is being sold for more money than the original sum.   **T   F**
    C. The client is not obliged to buy the goods when they arrive.   **T   F**
13. Applying Islamic banking principles, with *Murabaha*:
    A. The *Sharia'a* does not permit any financial penalty to be imposed on delinquent debtors.   **T   F**
    B. The client is obliged to purchase the assets, whereas under conventional bank lending they are not.   **T   F**
    C. There is no risk for the *Rab ul Mall* selling to Muslims.   **T   F**
14. The difference between *Murabaha* and *Ijara* is:
    A. With *Murabaha* the customer becomes the owner of the equipment from the first day of receiving it.   **T   F**
    B. With *Ijara* the customer becomes the owner of the equipment from the first day of receiving it.   **T   F**
    C. With *Murabaha* the customer becomes a debtor for the full price of the asset.   **T   F**
15. *Murabaha* is an Arabic term that means a 'deferred credit sale'.   **T   F**
16. *Murabaha* is an Arabic term that means a 'loan with a mutually agreed profit'.   **T   F**
17. One of the features of a *Murabaha* contract is that the seller discloses the cost price to the *Rab ul Mall*.   **T   F**

18. One of the features of a *Murabaha* contract is that a variable profit rate is added by the *Rab ul Mall*.   **T   F**
19. One of the features of a *Murabaha* contract is that the *Rab ul Mall,* or his agent, owns the product before selling it.   **T   F**
20. The *Sharia'a* ruling for a valid *Murabaha* sale is that the price the goods will be sold for is specified at a later date.   **T   F**
21. A *Rab ul Mall Murabaha* asset, after being bought, is owned by the *Rab ul Mall*.   **T   F**
22. A *Rab ul Mall Murabaha* asset, after being bought, is owned by the agent of the *Rab ul Mall*.   **T   F**
23. If there is default by a buyer, under a *Murabaha* contract, the *Rab ul Mall* can renegotiate the price with the buyer.   **T   F**
24. If there is default by a buyer, under a *Murabaha* contract, the *Rab ul Mall* can charge late payment fees.   **T   F**
25. If there is default by a buyer, under a *Murabaha* contract, the buyer can be obliged to pay money to charity.   **T   F**
26. A key feature of the *Murabaha* contract is that money is being sold for money.   **T   F**
27. A key feature of a *Murabaha* contract is that a commodity is being sold for money.   **T   F**
28. A key feature of a *Murabaha* contract is that a commodity is being sold for a commodity.   **T   F**
29. With a *Murabaha* contract, no price renegotiation by the *Rab ul Mall* is permitted.   **T   F**
30. With a *Murabaha* contract the price to the buyer is fixed.   **T   F**
31. What makes *Murabaha Sharia'a* compliant is that the *Rab ul Mall* is selling goods for money on a spot basis.   **T   F**
32. What makes *Murabaha Sharia'a* compliant is that money is being sold for more money than the original sum.   **T   F**
33. What makes *Murabaha Sharia'a* compliant is that a client is not obliged to buy the goods when the agent receives them.   **T   F**
34. One difference between *Murabaha* and *Ijara* is that with a *Murabaha* contract the customer becomes the owner of the goods from the day he receives them.   **T   F**
35. One difference between *Murabaha* and *Ijara* is that with an *Ijara* contract the customer becomes the owner of the goods from the day they receive them.   **T   F**
36. One difference between *Murabaha* and *Ijara* is that with a *Murabaha* contract the customer becomes a debtor for the full price of the equipment.   **T   F**
37. Under a *Murabaha* contract, the *Rab ul Mall* is exposed to a total loss of capital.   **T   F**
38. Under a *Murabaha* contract, the *Rab ul Mall* is exposed to no loss of capital.   **T   F**
39. Under a *Murabaha* contract, the *Rab ul Mall* is at risk for the entire period of the contract.   **T   F**
40. Under a *Murabaha* contract, the *Rab ul Mall* is at risk for a short period only.   **T   F**
41. Under a *Murabaha* contract, the *Rab ul Mall* is at risk until *al-muslam* is delivered.   **T   F**
42. Under a *Murabaha* contract, the *Rab ul Mall* is at risk even after the contract has expired.   **T   F**
43. *Murabaha* is a *Sharia'a*-compliant Islamic mode of finance because the risk is such that if the manufacturer, who has agreed to manufacture the goods, makes faulty goods or does not deliver them on time, the *Rab ul Mall* is at risk.   **T   F**
44. *Murabaha* is basically the sale of goods at a price covering the cost of purchase minus a margin of profit agreed upon by both parties concerned.   **T   F**

45. *Murabaha* is basically the sale of goods at a price covering the cost of purchase plus a margin of profit agreed upon by both parties concerned.   **T   F**
46. The possibility of having a *Sharia'a*-compliant *Murabaha*-based *sukuk* (bond) is only possible in the primary market.   **T   F**
47. The negotiability of *Murabaha sukuk* or their trading in the secondary market is illegal, due to the fact that it is illegal in the *Sharia'a* to trade debt for debt, on a deferred basis, at prices different from the par value.   **T   F**
48. Despite the fact that *Murabaha* instruments are debt instruments, it is permissible to sell these instruments if mixed with other assets, provided that the real assets and services proportions are significantly smaller than the debt and cash proportions.   **T   F**
49. Despite the fact that *Murabaha* instruments are debt instruments, it is permissible to sell these instruments if mixed with other assets provided that the real assets and services proportions are significantly larger than the debt and cash proportions.   **T   F**
50. With a *Murabaha* contract, the *Rab ul Mall* has a completely certain rate of return.   **T   F**
51. With a *Murabaha* contract the *Rab ul Mall* has a completely uncertain rate of return.   **T   F**
52. With a *Murabaha* contract the *Rab ul Mall* has an uncertain rate of return for a short period only.   **T   F**
53. With a *Murabaha* contract the cost of capital, for the *Rab ul Mall*, is completely fixed and predetermined.   **T   F**
54. With a *Murabaha* contract the cost of capital, for the *Rab ul Mall*, is completely uncertain until the end of the contract.   **T   F**
55. *Murabaha* is a *Sharia'a*-compliant Islamic mode of finance because the risk is such that, if the *Rab ul Mall*'s client does not pay on time, or does not pay at all, the *Rab ul Mall* is at risk.   **T   F**
56. *Murabaha* is a *Sharia'a*-compliant Islamic mode of finance because the risk is such that the financial institution and the client have to share the losses in proportion to the respective capital contributions.   **T   F**
57. *Murabaha* is a *Sharia'a*-compliant Islamic mode of finance because the risk is such that if the leased asset is destroyed, without any misuse or negligence on the part of the lessee, it is the *Rab ul Mall* (lessor) who must bear the risk.   **T   F**
58. *Murabaha* is a *Sharia'a*-compliant Islamic mode of finance because the risk is such that if the *Rab ul Mall*'s client, who has been paid upfront, does not then deliver the goods at the agreed future date, there is the risk that the *Rab ul Mall* cannot easily resell the goods, exposing itself to risk.   **T   F**
59. Under a *Murabaha* contract the *Rab ul Mall* has no control over the management of the funds.   **T   F**
60. Under a *Murabaha* contract the *Rab ul Mall* has full control over the management of the funds.   **T   F**
61. *Murabaha* is a *Sharia'a*-compliant Islamic mode of finance because the risk is such that the *Rab ul Mall* can lose all his capital.   **T   F**

For Questions 62 to 71, only one of the potential answers is correct. Insert A, B or C where indicated below each question.

62. Which of the following is the most appropriate definition of *Murabaha*?
    A. *Murabaha* refers to an arrangement under which two or more partners share in investing in and receiving the profits from a partnership.

B. *Murabaha* refers to a contract for the sale of an item of property in which the seller declares his cost and adds an agreed profit and sells the item to the buyer at the cost plus an agreed profit.

C. *Murabaha* refers to a contract for the sale of goods in which the buyer pays the sales price of the goods in instalments.

✏ *Answer:*_____

63. A bank plans to enter into a *Murabaha* transaction with a client under which the bank will buy construction equipment from a manufacturer and sell it to the client, who will take delivery from the manufacturer and pay the bank the purchase price plus a profit over time. The bank also seeks a guarantee from the client of immediate repayment if the equipment is destroyed or lost. Is this guarantee permitted under the *Sharia'a*?

A. Yes, but only if the destruction or loss occurs after the client takes possession of the equipment.

B. Yes, but only if the destruction or loss is due to the wilful act or negligence of the client.

C. Yes, it is generally permitted to transfer such risk to the client, including if the risk occurs prior to the client taking possession of the equipment.

✏ *Answer:*_____

64. Assume that a financial firm participates in a *Musharaka* financing for a new venture together with three other financial firms. The new venture approaches the first financial firm for *Murabaha* financing for equipment it requires. Which of the following statements is most accurate?

A. The financial firm cannot provide the *Murabaha* financing because this would in effect provide it with a preferred return relative to the other financial firms.

B. The financial firm may provide the *Murabaha* financing, but because this would in effect provide it with a preferred return relative to the other financial firms, it must first obtain the approval of the other financial firms.

C. The financial firm may provide the *Murabaha* financing and the approval of the other financial firms is not required.

✏ *Answer:*_____

65. A potential banking client wants a bank to finance an equipment purchase from an equipment maker. Which of the following arrangements is most appropriate for this purpose?

A. In order to minimise risks, a *Murabaha* may be structured between a bank, equipment maker and client such that the equipment maker sells the equipment directly to the client and the bank directly pays the equipment maker.

B. A *Murabaha* transaction needs to be structured between a bank, equipment maker and client such that there are two sale contracts: one in which the equipment maker sells the equipment to the bank and one in which the bank sells the equipment to the client.

C. A *Murabaha* transaction needs to be structured between a bank, equipment maker and client such that there is one financing contract in which the bank finances the equipment maker's sale of the equipment to the client and one sale contract in which the equipment maker sells the equipment to the client.

✏ *Answer:*_____

66. A bank plans to enter into a *Murabaha* transaction with a client under which the bank will buy construction equipment from a manufacturer and resell it to the client, who will then take delivery from the manufacturer and pay the bank the purchase price plus a profit

over time. Is it permitted for the bank to require the client to directly take possession of the equipment from the manufacturer?

A. Yes, as long as legal title to the equipment first passes to the bank and then to the client.

B. Yes, as long as legal title to the equipment passes to the bank after the client takes possession of the equipment.

C. No, because the bank must take both legal title to, and physical possession of, the equipment before transferring possession to the client.

✒ *Answer:*_____

67. Which of the following statements most accurately describes what can be financed in a *Murabaha* transaction?

A. A *Murabaha* transaction may involve the financing of real property (land), fixtures, moveable property, intellectual property or financial assets (such as accounts receivable).

B. A *Murabaha* transaction may involve the financing of tangible assets such as real property (land), fixtures and moveable property but not intangible assets such as intellectual property nor financial assets (such as accounts receivable).

C. A *Murabaha* transaction may involve the financing of tangible assets such as real property (land), fixtures, moveable property and intangible assets such as financial assets (such as accounts receivable) but not intellectual property.

✒ *Answer:*_____

68. A bank's client wishes to engage an equipment maker to manufacture some specialised equipment. The equipment maker requires some advance financing and the client approaches the bank for financing. Which of the following statements is most accurate in this contract?

A. This transaction may not be financed under Islamic legal principles because the subject matter is not in existence at the proposed time of financing.

B. This transaction may be financed as a *Murabaha* transaction involving one sale contract between the equipment maker and the bank and a sale contract between the bank and the client.

C. This transaction may be financed as an *Istisna'a* between the bank and equipment maker and a *Murabaha* between the bank and the client.

✒ *Answer:*_____

69. In a *Murabaha* financing transaction, a bank buys a commodity and sells the commodity to its client for the purchase price and an agreed mark-up. If the market price of the commodity goes up or down before the client completes payment, does the bank need to adjust its agreed mark-up?

A. Yes, because otherwise there would be no commodity price risk to the bank.

B. Yes, but the bank's risk in the case of a fall in the price of the commodity is limited to the amount of the agreed mark-up.

C. No, because the bank has sold the commodity to the client after purchasing it. Like any other seller, the bank no longer has exposure to the after-sales price of the commodity.

✒ *Answer:*_____

70. Which of the following statements most accurately describes the general opinion about Islamically acceptable fines and penalties for financing with *Murabaha* and *Ijara*?

A. Almost all scholars agree that when financing with *Murabaha* and *Ijara*, if the party responsible for making payment does not make the required payment at the stipulated time, the financing party cannot be entitled to a fine or late payment penalty.

    B. Almost all scholars agree that when financing with *Murabaha* and *Ijara*, if the party responsible for making payment does not make the required payment at the stipulated time, the financing party may be entitled to a fine or late payment penalty.

    C. When financing with *Murabaha* and *Ijara*, scholars are divided on whether the financing party may be entitled to a fine or late payment penalty if the party responsible for making payment does not make the required payment at the stipulated time.

    ✎ *Answer:*_____

71. Three potential partners decide to open a bakery business. Two of the partners are only able to contribute a small amount of capital but are willing to manage the enterprise. The third partner is wealthy and can contribute substantial capital but cannot devote any management time. Which form of financing is the most appropriate for them to use?

    A. *Murabaha* is the most appropriate. The wealthy person should purchase the plant and equipment and sell it for profit to the enterprise, with the other two providing working capital. The wealthy person cannot obtain an equity share in the enterprise because there is the risk he could abuse his position.

    B. As all three are willing to contribute capital *Musharaka* is most appropriate, with the two smaller investors also managing the enterprise.

    C. *Mudaraba* is the most appropriate, but all the equity capital must come from one person. The others may receive a share of profits but cannot also invest capital.

    ✎ *Answer:*_____

4.2.3 Risks with the *Murabaha* Contract

Describe at least two risks associated with the *Murabaha* contract.

Risk 1

✎ _____

_____

_____

_____

_____

_____

Risk 2

✎ _____

_____

_____

_____

_____

_____

4.3 ANSWERS

4.3.1   What are the Features of the *Murabaha* Contract?

1. How does it work?

   The bank purchases the commodity for the client. The goods can be capital goods, consumable goods or raw materials

   No money is advanced by the banker to the buyer. The bank sells the goods to the client at a higher price.

2. In what sense is *Murabaha* an asset-based or equity-based source of finance?

   Money has no intrinsic utility in Islam; it is only a medium of exchange. Profit dealing through money is *riba* and therefore *haram*. Financing in Islam must be asset based or equity based. Any asset created must be intrinsically illiquid. As it says in the *Qur'an*: 'Allah has permitted trade and prohibited *riba*'.

   The bank must buy real assets. As the banker is creating inventory, *Murabaha* is asset based.

3. What is the risk for the *Rab ul Mall* providing the finance?

   Islam requires that any profits are only justified if there is risk preference by investors. This is based on the Arabic term *Al Ghunm bil-Ghurm*, i.e., profits must be linked with the investors' willingness to take risk.

   The selling price remains fixed. If the seller does not pay on time there is a risk. There is also the risk that the customer does not pay at all.

4.3.2   The *Murabaha* Contract

4. A. TRUE
   B. TRUE
   C. FALSE
5. A. TRUE
   B. FALSE
   C. TRUE
6. A. TRUE
   B. FALSE
   C. TRUE
7. A. TRUE
   B. FALSE
   C. FALSE
8. A. FALSE
   B. FALSE
   C. TRUE
9. A. FALSE
   B. TRUE
   C. FALSE
10. A. TRUE
    B. TRUE
    C. TRUE
    D. TRUE

11. A. TRUE
    B. TRUE
    C. TRUE
    D. TRUE
12. A. TRUE
    B. FALSE
    C. TRUE
13. A. TRUE
    B. FALSE
    C. FALSE
14. A. TRUE
    B. FALSE
    C. TRUE
15. TRUE
16. FALSE
17. TRUE
18. FALSE
19. TRUE
20. FALSE
21. FALSE
22. TRUE
23. FALSE
24. FALSE
25. TRUE
26. FALSE
27. TRUE
28. FALSE
29. TRUE
30. TRUE
31. FALSE
32. FALSE
33. TRUE
34. TRUE
35. FALSE
36. TRUE
37. TRUE
38. FALSE
39. FALSE
40. TRUE
41. FALSE
42. FALSE
43. FALSE
44. FALSE
45. TRUE
46. TRUE
47. TRUE
48. FALSE

49. TRUE
50. FALSE
51. FALSE
52. TRUE
53. TRUE
54. FALSE
55. TRUE
56. FALSE
57. FALSE
58. FALSE
59. FALSE
60. TRUE
61. FALSE
62. B
63. C
64. C
65. B
66. A
67. A
68. C
69. C
70. C
71. B

4.3.3   Risks with the *Murabaha* Contract

Describe at least two risks for banks providing the *Murabaha* contract

Risk 1 *Credit Risk*: Customer may not be able to honour the payment obligation.

Risk 2 *Market Risk*: If it is a nonbinding *Murabaha*, the customer can cancel the agreement. The bank then has to sell the goods in the open market.

5
The *Mudaraba* Contract as a Mode of Islamic Finance

5.1 LEARNING OUTCOMES, SUMMARY OVERVIEW AND PROBLEMS

5.1.1 Learning Outcomes

After reading Chapter 5 you should be able to do the following:

* Define *Mudaraba*.
* Explain the treatment of money within Islam.
* Distinguish a conventional loan from *Mudaraba*.
* Describe the elements of a *Mudaraba* transaction.
* Contrast *Mudaraba* with the other modes of Islamic finance.
* Describe the different types of *Mudaraba*.
* Identify the Arabic terminology used in *Mudaraba*.
* Explain the practicalities of implementing *Mudaraba*.
* Identify the reasoning behind the *Sharia'a* rulings on *Mudaraba*.
* Explain the practicalities of implementing two-tier *Mudaraba*.
* Describe the *Sharia'a* rulings on *Mudaraba*.
* Identify problems with applying *Mudaraba*.
* Explain the importance of deferred sales within Islamic finance.
* Identify the deferred sale versus profit and loss share (PLS) contracts.
* Test that you have fully understood the principles that underlie the *Mudaraba* contract.

5.1.2 Summary Overview

Mudaraba refers to an investment, on the customers behalf, by a bank. It takes the form of a contract between two parties, one providing the funds and the other providing the expertise, who agree to the division of any profits made in advance. In other words, the bank would make *Sharia'a*-compliant investments and share the profits with the customer, in effect charging for the time and effort. If no profit is made, the loss is borne by the customer and the bank takes no fee.

Mudaraba is a contract whereby one side (the investor or *Rab ul Mall*) contributes money and the other side (the manager or *Mudarib*) does the work. The *Rab ul Mall* bears all losses, and the *Mudarib* earns a profit share, if the project is profitable.

Mudaraba can be understood as being similar to the function of an asset manager.

Legally the *Mudaraba* contract is established as being permissible by the consensus of the Islamic scholars and is not based on primary sources of the *Sharia'a*.

As the profits are shared with the manager (*Mudarib*) and the capital provider (*Rab ul Mall*), but the losses are borne only by the capital provider, the *Mudaraba* mode is also named 'profit sharing – loss bearing'. Before the manager gets his share, the losses (if any), however, need to be recovered. A wage could be negotiated.

5.1.2.1   *Restricted versus Unrestricted* Mudaraba

Capital can be provided on an unrestricted basis for any purpose that the manager deems fitting (an unrestricted *Mudaraba* is called a *Mudaraba al Mutlaqah*). Capital can also be granted with conditions as to what the funds can be invested in: the latter is technically called restricted *Mudaraba* (*Mudaraba al Muqayyadah*).

5.1.2.2   *Two-tier* Mudaraba

Two-tier *Mudaraba* was the initial concept for Islamic banking. The structure is set up so that the Islamic bank is engaged in two different *Mudaraba* transactions, one with depositors and one with those to whom it provides financing. The first *Mudaraba* is between the bank and the client having surplus capital (depositors) and the second one is between the bank and the clients who require financing.

The first-tier *Mudaraba* between depositors and the Islamic bank has depositors acting as *Rab ul Mall* and the bank acting as the *Mudarib*. The depositors place their funds with the bank with no guarantee of return of the principal and a return based on the profitability of the investments made by the bank on their behalf. As with other *Mudaraba*, the depositors bear any losses and share profits with the Islamic bank according to a pre-agreed ratio.

The second-tier *Mudaraba* between the Islamic bank and those receiving financing has the bank acting as *Rab ul Mall* and the customer acting as *Mudarib*. The bank bears all losses except in cases of fraud by the *Mudarib* and shares profits with the customer according to a pre-agreed ratio.

The concept was developed by Islamic economists as a credible alternative to saving accounts. So in a two-tier *Mudaraba*, the bank provides an intermediation role between depositors and customers needing financing and is expected to be able to achieve sufficient diversification and use its greater resources to protect depositors more adequately from risks associated with each individual second-tier *Mudaraba* agreement. However, because the Islamic bank retains liability for all losses, which are then passed along to depositors, it suffers from an informational asymmetry that has limited *Mudaraba* use in practice.

Another problem with the two-tier *Mudaraba* model is that not only do depositors have their principal at risk, but also they are likely to see significant swings in the profits paid on their deposits. One solution to the latter problem is to smooth profits across time using a profit reserve, which could lower the volatility for the depositors.

5.1.2.3   *Problems and Risks*

One of the major drawbacks of the *Mudaraba* mode of finance is that there is no legal framework in the contemporary commercial laws of most countries, especially non-Islamic countries, which can be relied upon in the case of a dispute. As such the *Mudaraba* Agreement must be comprehensive and must cover all the details.

The other major shortcoming is that to specify a time limit (timeframe) in the *Mudaraba* makes it null and void because the principle of *Mudaraba* is that it continues until the other partner completes the work for which the agreement has been established and its proceeds are collected. This, of course, leads the bank to have difficulties planning the actual cash flow and profit accrual and it would therefore be advisable to deal with *Mudaraba* as either a medium- or long-term investment, even though it may be possible to conclude it earlier.

There is a *Sharia'a* ruling that it is not permissible for the bank to interfere in the running of the work in order to administer the execution of the project. The bank will normally only use contractors with which it has full confidence regarding their honesty and technical capabilities. This is difficult to achieve without examining all aspects of the contract and the contractor.

In addition, the bank must have, or endeavour to establish, the technical capability to carry out the necessary duties, exercise due diligence and make the proper credit and technical follow-up to ensure that the project execution is going according to schedule. It is also advisable to have contingency plans and strategies for intervening in the event that the contractor fails to carry out its commitments.

Islamic banks need to be aware of, and mitigate against, the risk of wrongful use of funds. To do so, they establish a drawdown mechanism that ensures that the funds are spent on the project itself and not any other work that the contractor may be carrying out at the same time.

A mismatch between the amount of money withdrawn and the completed work could happen. This may lead to over-spending at the end of the contract, especially if the contractor is not using all the money for the specific project (the subject of the *Mudaraba*) or not properly managing the spending. In either case the bank must step in to correct the situation as soon as it notices any indication of such mismatch.

Project cancellation completely or partially may also happen during the course of the project. To ensure that the bank's investment is not lost, it should ensure that it is aware of all developments throughout the life of the project and has direct access to the project owner. In addition, careful monitoring of spending will help in minimising the bank's losses.

Project withdrawal may take place, especially when the contractor is accused of major negligence. Therefore, the *Mudaraba* Agreement must cover this possibility and also be clear and specific in terms of how such a situation be dealt with, bearing in mind that in the *Mudaraba* Agreement the contractor is not responsible or accountable for losses or damages that are beyond his control. In such cases the bank risks losing its money unless it can prove that the contractor is negligent and, as such, is responsible for such loss.

In conclusion, *Mudaraba* can be used as a type or mode of finance that is heavily dependent on the bank accepting the performance risk of the contractor to perform the work successfully within the project's budget and timeframe limitations.

The *Mudaraba* Agreement must be comprehensive and detailed in order to cover all aspects of the work and how to deal with each possible risk that may occur. The financial structuring should be appropriate to the type of project in hand in order to minimise the possibility of mismatch between spending and work completion and misappropriation of funds.

Mudaraba is not without risk, and its success largely depends on how well the bank manages this risk. Therefore the bank must examine all matters that are directly or indirectly related to the project: the contractor, the project owner and any matter that may have positive or negative future influences on the project or the agreement.

5.2 QUESTIONS

5.2.1   What are the Features of the *Mudaraba* Contract?

1. How does *Mudaraba* work?

    ✎ _____

    _____

    _____

    _____

2. In what sense is *Mudaraba* an asset-based or equity-based source of finance?

    ✎ _____

    _____

    _____

    _____

3. What is the risk for the *Rab ul Mall* providing the finance?

    ✎ _____

    _____

    _____

    _____

5.2.2   The *Mudaraba* Contract

Circle true (T) or false (F) in the statements below. Note: you need to indicate T or F for each statement.

4. *Mudaraba* is an Arabic term that means:
   A. A deferred credit sale.   **T   F**
   B. 'Journeying through the earth seeking the bounty of Allah'.   **T   F**
   C. 'Journeying through the earth as a form of *Hajj*'.   **T   F**
5. *Mudaraba* can be used in the following senses:
   A. A relationship between a depositor and the *Rab ul Mall*.   **T   F**
   B. A relationship between the *Rab ul Mall* and the parties to whom the finance is provided.   **T   F**
   C. A relationship between the shareholders and the depositor.   **T   F**
6. *Rab ul Mall* refers to:
   A. The working partner.   **T   F**
   B. The investor.   **T   F**
   C. The *Sharia'a* scholar.   **T   F**
7. The *Mudarib* is:
   A. The investor.   **T   F**
   B. The working partner.   **T   F**
   C. The *Sharia'a* scholar.   **T   F**

8. *Mudaraba* is sometimes called:
   A. A full partnership.   **T   F**
   B. A silent partnership.   **T   F**
   C. A joint stock company.   **T   F**
9. The *Rab ul Mall* provides:
   A. The entire capital for the project.   **T   F**
   B. No capital for the project.   **T   F**
   C. Some capital for the project.   **T   F**
10. The *Mudarib* provides:
    A. Some of the work for the project.   **T   F**
    B. All the work for the project.   **T   F**
    C. No work for the project.   **T   F**
11. Profits are always shared:
    A. At a ratio of 50:50.   **T   F**
    B. According to a pre-agreed ratio.   **T   F**
    C. At a ratio that varies depending upon the profitability of the contract.   **T   F**
12. Financial losses are always:
    A. Shared in a fixed ratio.   **T   F**
    B. Paid by the *Rab ul Mall*.   **T   F**
    C. Paid by the *Mudarib*.   **T   F**
13. Given the investment split between the *Rab ul Mall* and the *Mudarib*, illustrated below, indicate the *Sharia'a*-compliant profit and loss share potentially agreed:

	Investment contribution	Profit share agreed	Loss share agreed	
A	70/30	60/40	70/30	T F
B	60/40	70/30	70/30	T F
C	100/0	60/40	90/10	T F
D	100/0	60/40	70/30	T F
E	100/0	30/70	100/0	T F
F	100/0	60/40	100/0	T F

14. The liability of the *Mudarib* is limited to:
    A. Any financial losses made.   **T   F**
    B. Any time and work contributed.   **T   F**
    C. Depends on the agreement.   **T   F**
15. Under Tier 1 *Mudaraba*:
    A. The depositor is the *Rab ul Mall*.   **T   F**
    B. The *Rab ul Mall* contributes capital and no expertise.   **T   F**
    C. The *Mudarib* contributes capital and no expertise.   **T   F**
16. Under Tier 2 *Mudaraba*:
    A. The *Rab ul Mall* is the Islamic bank.   **T   F**
    B. The *Rab ul Mall* contributes capital and no expertise.   **T   F**
    C. The *Mudarib* contributes capital and no expertise.   **T   F**
17. The difference between *Mudaraba* and *Musharaka* is:
    A. *Musharaka* involves limited liability.   **T   F**
    B. *Mudaraba* involves unlimited liability.   **T   F**
    C. *Musharaka* involves unlimited liability.   **T   F**

18. The difference between *Musharaka* and *Mudaraba* is:
    A. Risks and returns in *Musharaka* are shared in proportion to the capital invested. **T F**
    B. Investment in *Mudaraba* comes only from the *Rab ul Mall*. **T F**
    C. All the partners in *Musharaka* share any loss in proportion to the extent of their investment. **T F**
    D. Any losses in *Mudaraba* are suffered by the *Rab ul Mall* alone. **T F**
19. Restricted *Mudaraba* means:
    A. Investments are restricted to *halal* activities. **T F**
    B. Investments are directed to specific investments. **T F**
    C. The *Rab ul Mall* can invest in profitable investments of its choice. **T F**
20. Unrestricted *Mudaraba* means:
    A. The *Rab ul Mall* can invest in profitable investments of its choice. **T F**
    B. The *Rab ul Mall* can invest in *haram* activities. **T F**
    C. The *Rab ul Mall*'s funds can be co-mingled with the funds of the depositors. **T F**
21. Unrestricted *Mudaraba* means:
    A. There are no constraints on the activities of the *Rab ul Mall*. **T F**
    B. That depositors funds cannot be co-mingled with those of the *Rab ul Mall*. **T F**
    C. That profits and losses are shared with depositors. **T F**
22. *Mudaraba* is an Arabic term that means a 'deferred credit sale'. **T F**
23. *Mudaraba* is used in the sense of a relationship between a depositor and the *Sharia'a*. **T F**
24. *Mudaraba* cannot be used in the sense of a relationship between the *Rab ul Mall* and the parties to whom the finance is provided. **T F**
25. With a *Mudaraba* contract the term *Rab ul Mall* means the working partner. **T F**
26. With a *Mudaraba* contract the term *Rab ul Mall* means the investor. **T F**
27. With a *Mudaraba* contract the *Mudarib* is the investor. **T F**
28. With a *Mudaraba* contract the *Mudarib* is the working partner. **T F**
29. *Mudaraba* is sometimes called a 'full partnership'. **T F**
30. *Mudaraba* is sometimes called a 'silent partnership'. **T F**
31. With a *Mudaraba* contract the *Rab ul Mall* provides the entire capital for the project. **T F**
32. With a *Mudaraba* contract the *Rab ul Mall* provides no capital for the project. **T F**
33. With a *Mudaraba* contract the *Rab ul Mall* provides some of the capital for the project. **T F**
34. With a *Mudaraba* contract the *Mudarib* provides some of the work for the project. **T F**
35. With a *Mudaraba* contract the *Mudarib* provides all the work for the project. **T F**
36. Profits, under a *Mudaraba* contract, are always shared in the ratio of 50:50. **T F**
37. Profits, under a *Mudaraba* contract, are always shared according to a pre-agreed ratio. **T F**
38. Financial losses, under a *Mudaraba* contract, are always shared according to a fixed ratio. **T F**
39. Financial losses, under a *Mudaraba* contract, are always paid by the *Rab ul Mall*. **T F**
40. Financial losses, under a *Mudaraba* contract, are always paid by the *Mudarib*. **T F**
41. The liability of the *Mudarib*, under a *Mudaraba* contract, is to any financial losses made. **T F**
42. The liability of the *Mudarib*, under a *Mudaraba* contract, is to his time and work contributed. **T F**

43. Under a *Mudaraba* contract the *Rab ul Mall* contributes capital and no expertise.   **T   F**
44. One difference between a *Mudaraba* and *Musharaka* is that a *Musharaka* contract involves unlimited liability.   **T   F**
45. Under a *Mudaraba* contract the *Mudarib* contributes capital and no expertise.   **T   F**
46. One difference between *Mudaraba* and *Musharaka*, is that a *Musharaka* contract involves limited liability.   **T   F**
47. One difference between *Mudaraba* and *Musharaka*, is that a *Mudaraba* contract involves unlimited liability.   **T   F**
48. One difference between *Mudaraba* and *Musharaka*, is that a *Mudaraba* contract involves limited liability.   **T   F**
49. One difference between *Musharaka* and *Mudaraba* is that risks and returns, in a *Musharaka* contract, are shared in proportion to the capital invested.   **T   F**
50. One difference between *Musharaka* and *Mudaraba*, is that investment, in a *Mudaraba* contract, comes only from the *Rab ul Mall*.   **T   F**
51. One difference between *Musharaka* and *Mudaraba*, is that, in a *Musharaka* contract, all the partners share any losses, to the extent of the ratio of their investment.   **T   F**
52. One difference between *Musharaka* and *Mudaraba*, is that, in a *Mudaraba* contract, any losses are suffered by the *Rab ul Mall* alone.   **T   F**
53. With an unrestricted *Mudaraba* contract the *Rab ul Mall* can invest in profitable investments of its choice.   **T   F**
54. With an unrestricted *Mudaraba* contract the *Rab ul Mall*'s funds can be co-mingled with the funds of the depositor.   **T   F**
55. Under a *Mudaraba* contract the *Rab ul Mall* is at risk for the entire period of the contract.   **T   F**
56. Under a *Mudaraba* contract the *Rab ul Mall* is at risk for a short period only.   **T   F**
57. With a *Mudaraba* contract the *Rab ul Mall* has a completely uncertain rate of return.   **T   F**
58. With a *Mudaraba* contract the *Rab ul Mall* has a completely certain rate of return.   **T   F**
59. With a *Mudaraba* contract the *Rab ul Mall* has an uncertain rate of return for a short period only.   **T   F**
60. The *Mudarib* must take responsibility for a poor *Mudaraba* performance if this is due to a legal cause of liability, such as the *Mudarib* being negligent or having done something dishonest leading to losses.   **T   F**
61. The *Rab ul Mall* must take responsibility for a poor *Mudaraba* performance even if this is due to a legal cause of liability, such as the *Mudarib* being negligent or having done something dishonest leading to losses.   **T   F**
62. If the *Mudarib* guarantees the capital or a fixed profit from a *Mudaraba* contract this would be considered valid under the *Sharia'a*.   **T   F**
63. *Mudaraba* is basically the sale of goods at a price covering the cost of purchase minus a margin of profit agreed upon by both parties concerned.   **T   F**
64. Given the investment contribution in a *Mudaraba* contract between the *Rab ul Mall* and the partner, as outlined below, the following is the *Sharia'a*-compliant profit/loss share that could have been agreed:

Investment contribution	Profit share agreed	Loss share agreed
100/0	60/40	100/0

T   F

65. With a *Mudaraba* contract the cost of capital, for the *Rab ul Mall*, is completely fixed and predetermined.   **T   F**

66. With a *Mudaraba* contract the cost of capital, for the *Rab ul Mall*, is completely uncertain until the end of the contract.   **T   F**

67. Given the investment contribution in a *Mudaraba* contract between the *Rab ul Mall* and the partner as outlined below, the following is the *Sharia'a*-compliant profit/loss share that could have been agreed:

Investment contribution	Profit share agreed	Loss share agreed
70/30	60/40	70/30

T F

68. Given the investment contribution in a *Mudaraba* contract between the *Rab ul Mall* and the partner as outlined below, the following is the *Sharia'a*-compliant profit/loss share that could have been agreed:

Investment contribution	Profit share agreed	Loss share agreed
60/40	70/30	70/30

T F

69. Given the investment contribution in a *Mudaraba* contract between the *Rab ul Mall* and the partner as outlined below, the following is the *Sharia'a*-compliant profit/loss share that could have been agreed:

Investment contribution	Profit share agreed	Loss share agreed
100/0	60/40	90/10

T F

70. *Mudaraba* is a *Sharia'a*-compliant Islamic mode of finance because the risk is such that, under a profit and loss sharing contract, the *Rab ul Mall* can lose all his capital and the *Mudarib* can only lose the time and effort expended.   **T   F**

71. *Mudaraba* is a *Sharia'a*-compliant Islamic mode of finance because the risk is such that if the *Rab ul Mall*'s client does not pay on time, or does not pay at all, the *Rab ul Mall* is at risk.   **T   F**

72. *Mudaraba* is a *Sharia'a*-compliant Islamic mode of finance because the risk is such that if the leased asset is destroyed, without any misuse or negligence on the part of the lessee, it is the *Rab ul Mall* (lessor) who must bear the risk.   **T   F**

73. *Mudaraba* is a *Sharia'a*-compliant Islamic mode of finance because the risk is such that if the manufacturer, who has agreed to manufacture the goods, makes faulty goods or does not deliver them on time, the *Rab ul Mall* is at risk.   **T   F**

74. *Mudaraba* is a *Sharia'a*-compliant Islamic mode of finance because the risk is such that if the *Rab ul Mall*'s client, who has been paid upfront, does not then deliver at the agreed future date, there is the risk that the *Rab ul Mall* cannot easily resell the goods, exposing itself to risk .   **T   F**

75. Given the investment contribution in a *Mudaraba* contract between the *Rab ul Mall* and the partner as outlined below, the following is the *Sharia'a*-compliant profit/loss share that could have been agreed:

Investment contribution	Profit share	Loss share agreed
100/0	60/40	70/30

T F

76. Given the investment contribution in a *Mudaraba* contract between the *Rab ul Mall* and the partner, as outlined below, the following is the *Sharia'a*-compliant profit/loss share that could have been agreed:

Investment contribution	Profit share agreed	Loss share agreed
100/0	30/70	100/0

T F

77. Under a *Mudaraba* contract the *Rab ul Mall* has no control over the management of the funds. **T F**
78. Under a *Mudaraba* contract the *Rab ul Mall* has full control over the management of the funds. **T F**
79. Under a *Mudaraba* contract the *Rab ul Mall* is exposed to a total loss of the capital invested. **T F**
80. Under a *Mudaraba* contract the *Rab ul Mall* is exposed to no loss of the capital invested. **T F**
81. Under a *Mudaraba* contract the *Rab ul Mall* is at risk until the project is finished. **T F**
82. *Mudaraba* is a *Sharia'a*-compliant mode of finance given that the risk is such that the financial institution and the client, under a profit and loss share contract, have to share the losses in proportion to their respective capital contributions. **T F**
83. Under a *Mudaraba* contract the *Rab ul Mall* is at risk even after the contract has expired. **T F**

5.2.3 *Musharaka* versus the *Mudaraba* Contract

84. *Musharaka* is an Arabic term that means a 'deferred credit sale'. **T F**
85. *Musharaka* is an Arabic term that means 'a joint enterprise formed for conducting a business'. **T F**
86. *Musharaka* is sometimes called a 'silent partnership'. **T F**
87. *Musharaka* is sometimes called a 'full partnership'. **T F**
88. With a *Musharaka* contract, profits are shared in proportion to the amount invested. **T F**
89. With a *Musharaka* contract, profits are shared according to a pre-agreed specific ratio. **T F**
90. With a *Musharaka* contract, profits are shared in the ratio of 50:50. **T F**
91. With a *Musharaka* contract, losses are shared according to the proportion of the amount invested. **T F**

92. With a *Musharaka* contract, losses are shared according to the same agreed ratio as profits.   **T   F**
93. With a *Musharaka* contract, losses are shared in the ratio of 50:50.   **T   F**
94. One difference between *Musharaka* and *Mudaraba* is that a *Musharaka* contract involves limited liability.   **T   F**
95. One difference between *Musharaka* and *Mudaraba* is that a *Mudaraba* contract involves unlimited liability.   **T   F**
96. One difference between *Musharaka* and *Mudaraba* is that a *Musharaka* contract involves unlimited liability.   **T   F**
97. One difference between *Musharaka* and *Mudaraba* is that returns, in a *Musharaka* contract, are based on the proportion of the capital invested.   **T   F**
98. One difference between *Musharaka* and *Mudaraba* is that losses, in a *Musharaka* contract, are shared in proportion to the capital invested.   **T   F**
99. One difference between *Musharaka* and *Mudaraba* is that investment, in a *Mudaraba* contract, comes only from the *Rab ul Mall*.   **T   F**
100. One difference between *Musharaka* and *Mudaraba* is that, in a *Musharaka* contract, all the partners share the loss in proportion to the ratio of their investment.   **T   F**
101. One difference between *Musharaka* and *Mudaraba* is that, in a *Mudaraba* contract, any losses are suffered by the *Rab ul Mall* alone.   **T   F**

For Questions 102 to 103, only one of the potential answers is correct. Insert A, B or C where indicated below each question.

102. Which of the following is the most appropriate definition of *Mudaraba*?
  A. *Mudaraba* refers to a contract for the sale of an item of property in which the seller declares his cost and adds an agreed profit and sells the item to the buyer at the cost plus an agreed profit.
  B. *Mudaraba* refers to a form of contract in which one party contributes capital and the other party contributes entrepreneurial effort to a business venture. The proportionate share in profit from the business venture is determined by mutual agreement.
  C. *Mudaraba* refers to a form of business contract in which both parties contribute capital and personal effort to a business venture. The proportionate share in profit from the business venture is determined by mutual agreement.
  *Answer:*_____

103. Which of the following statements most accurately depicts the difference or similarity between *Mudaraba* and *Musharaka*?
  A. In a *Mudaraba* transaction, the financing party typically does not play a role in management. In a *Musharaka* transaction, the financing party may play a role in management.
  B. In both *Mudaraba* and *Musharaka* transactions, the financing party typically plays a role in management.
  C. In a *Musharaka* transaction, the financing party typically does not play a role in management. In a *Mudaraba* transaction, the financing party may play a role in management.
  *Answer:*_____

5.2.4   Risks with the *Mudaraba* Contract

Describe at least two risks associated with the *Mudaraba* contract.

Risk 1

🖎 _____

_____

_____

_____

_____

_____

Risk 2

🖎 _____

_____

_____

_____

_____

_____

5.3 ANSWERS

5.3.1 What are the Features of the *Mudaraba* Contract?

1. How does *Mudaraba* work?

    The Islamic bank (*Rab ul Mall*) provides the borrower (*Mudarib*) with financial resources.

2. In what sense is *Mudaraba* an asset-based or equity-based source of finance?

    Money has no intrinsic utility in Islam; it is only a medium of exchange. Making profits from money is *riba* and thereby *haram*. Financing in Islam must be asset based or equity based. As it says in the *Qur'an*: 'Allah has permitted trade and prohibited *riba*'.

    Money is invested, with *Mudaraba*, for the purchase of real assets which will ultimately create wealth in the future, making it asset based and equity based.

3. What is the risk for the *Rab ul Mall* providing the finance?

    Islam requires that any profits are only justified if there is risk preference by investors. This is based on the Arabic term *Al Ghunm bil-Ghurm*, i.e., profits must be linked with the investors' willingness to take risk.

    The profits are shared between the parties in a proportion agreed in advance. Losses are the liability of the *Rab ul Mall*. The *Mudarib* risks losing only his expected share of profits. So there is risk for the *Rab ul Mall*.

5.3.2 The *Mudaraba* Contract

4. A. FALSE

    B. TRUE

    C. FALSE
5. A. TRUE
    B. TRUE
    C. FALSE
6. A. FALSE
    B. TRUE
    C. FALSE
7. A. FALSE
    B. TRUE
    C. FALSE
8. A. FALSE
    B. TRUE
    C. FALSE
9. A. TRUE
    B. FALSE
    C. FALSE
10. A. FALSE
    B. TRUE
    C. FALSE
11. A. FALSE
    B. TRUE
    C. FALSE
12. A. FALSE
    B. TRUE
    C. FALSE
13. A. FALSE
    B. FALSE
    C. FALSE
    D. FALSE
    E. TRUE
    F. TRUE
14. A. FALSE
    B. TRUE
    C. FALSE
15. A. TRUE
    B. TRUE
    C. FALSE
16. A. TRUE
    B. TRUE
    C. FALSE
17. A. FALSE
    B. FALSE
    C. TRUE
18. A. TRUE
    B. TRUE
    C. TRUE
    D. TRUE

19. A. FALSE
     B. TRUE
     C. FALSE
20. A. TRUE
     B. FALSE
     C. TRUE
21. A. FALSE
     B. FALSE
     C. TRUE
22. FALSE
23. FALSE
24. FALSE
25. FALSE
26. TRUE
27. FALSE
28. TRUE
29. FALSE
30. TRUE
31. TRUE
32. FALSE
33. FALSE
34. FALSE
35. TRUE
36. FALSE
37. TRUE
38. FALSE
39. TRUE
40. FALSE
41. FALSE
42. TRUE
43. TRUE
44. TRUE
45. FALSE
46. FALSE
47. FALSE
48. TRUE
49. TRUE
50. TRUE
51. TRUE
52. TRUE
53. TRUE
54. TRUE
55. TRUE
56. FALSE
57. TRUE
58. FALSE
59. FALSE

60. TRUE
61. FALSE
62. FALSE
63. FALSE
64. TRUE
65. FALSE
66. TRUE
67. FALSE
68. FALSE
69. FALSE
70. TRUE
71. FALSE
72. FALSE
73. FALSE
74. FALSE
75. FALSE
76. TRUE
77. TRUE
78. FALSE
79. TRUE
80. FALSE
81. TRUE
82. FALSE
83. FALSE

5.3.3 *Musharaka* versus the *Mudaraba* Contract

84. FALSE
85. TRUE
86. FALSE
87. TRUE
88. FALSE
89. TRUE
90. FALSE
91. TRUE
92. FALSE
93. FALSE
94. FALSE
95. FALSE
96. TRUE
97. FALSE
98. TRUE
99. TRUE
100. TRUE
101. TRUE
102. B
103. A

5.3.4   Risks with the *Mudaraba* Contract

Describe at least two risks for banks providing the *Mudaraba* contract.

Risk 1 *Displaced Commercial Risk*: The risk that the bank may retain investment account holder's funds by increasing the rate of return thus giving away its share of the profit.

Risk 2 *Credit Risk*: The risk that the entrepreneur/partner defaults and goes bankrupt.

6

The *Musharaka* Contract as a Mode of Islamic Finance

6.1   LEARNING OUTCOMES, SUMMARY OVERVIEW AND PROBLEMS

6.1.1   Learning Outcomes

After reading Chapter 6 you should be able to do the following:

- Define *Musharaka*.
- Distinguish a conventional loan from a *Musharaka* contract.
- Describe the elements of a *Musharaka* transaction.
- Contrast *Musharaka* with the other modes of Islamic finance.
- Identify the Arabic terminology used in *Musharaka*.
- Describe the different types of *Musharaka*.
- Identify the reasoning behind the *Sharia'a* rulings on *Musharaka*.
- Explain the practicalities of implementing *Musharaka*.
- Describe the *Sharia'a* rulings on *Musharaka*.
- Identify problems with applying *Musharaka*.
- Explain the importance of deferred sales within Islamic finance.
- Contrast the role of penalty defaults within conventional and Islamic finance.
- Explain how *Musharaka* can be used for home finance.
- Define LIBOR and explain its application with a *Musharaka* contract.
- Identify the deferred sale versus profit and loss share contracts.
- Test that you have fully understood the principles that underlie the *Musharaka* contract.

6.1.2   Summary Overview

Musharaka means partnership. It involves an investor placing capital with another person and both sharing the risk and reward (see Figure 6.1). The difference between *Musharaka* arrangements and conventional banking is that, with *Musharaka*, you can set any kind of profit sharing ratio, but losses must be proportionate to the amount invested.

The literal meaning of the word *Musharaka* is sharing. Under Islamic law, *Musharaka* refers to a joint partnership where two or more persons combine either their capital or labour, forming a business in which all partners share the profit according to a specific ratio, while the loss is shared according to the ratio of the contribution (meaning amount invested).

Musharaka is based on a mutual contract and, therefore, it needs to have the following features to enable it to be valid:

- Parties should be capable of entering into a contract (that is, they should be of legal age).
- The contract must take place with the free consent of the parties (without any duress).

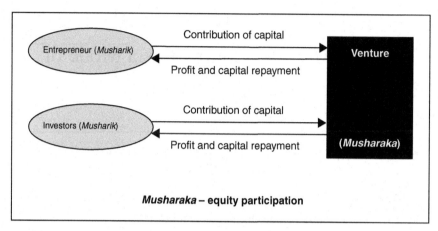

Figure 6.1 *Musharaka* flow chart

In *Musharaka*, every partner has a right to take part in the management, and to work for it. However, the partners may agree upon a condition where the management is carried out by one of them, and no other partner works for the *Musharaka*. In such a case the 'sleeping' (silent) partner is entitled to the profit only to the extent of his investment, and the ratio of profit allocated to him should not exceed the relative size of his investment in the business.

However, if all the partners agree to work for the joint venture, each one of them shall be treated as the agent of the other in all matters of business, and work done by any of them in the normal course of business is deemed as being authorised by all partners.

Musharaka can take the form of an unlimited, unrestricted and equal partnership in which the partners enjoy complete equality in the areas of capital, management and right of disposition. In this case each partner is both the agent and guarantor of the other.

Another more limited investment partnership is also available. This type of partnership occurs when two or more parties contribute to a capital fund with money, contributions in kind or labour. In this case each partner is only the agent and not the guarantor of his partner.

For both forms, the partners share profits in an agreed upon manner and bear losses in proportion to the size of their capital contributions.

The conventional notion of 'interest' predetermines a fixed rate of return on a loan advanced by the financier irrespective of the profit earned or loss suffered by the debtor, whereas *Musharaka* does not envisage a fixed rate of return. Instead, the return in *Musharaka* is based on the actual profit earned by the joint venture. The presence of risk in *Musharaka* makes it acceptable as an Islamic financing instrument. The financier in an interest-bearing loan cannot normally suffer a loss, while the financier in *Musharaka* can suffer a loss if the joint venture fails to produce fruits.

6.1.2.1   Musharaka *as used for Home Financing*

When used in home financing *Musharaka* is applied as a diminishing partnership. In home financing, the customer forms a partnership with the financial institution for the purchase of a property. The financial institution rents out its part of the property to the client and receives compensation in the form of rent, which is based on a mutually agreed fair market value. Any

Table 6.1 Example of payment schedule for a home-loan under *Musharaka*.

Month	Rent (US$)	Extra payment (US$)	Total fixed payments (US$)	Bank's ownership (US$)
Opening				120,000
1	800	347	1147	119,653
2	798	349	1147	119,304
...	...	...	...	...
176	37	1110	1147	4439
177	30	1117	1147	3322
178	22	1125	1147	2197
179	15	1132	1147	1065
180	7	1065	1072	0

amount paid above the rental value increases the customer's share in the property and reduces the share of the financial institution.

The application of diminishing *Musharaka* with home financing can be illustrated with the help of the following example, provided by LaRiba bank in the US.

Assume that a potential buyer is interested in purchasing a home worth US$150,000. The buyer approaches an Islamic financial institution for the purchase of the property and puts down 20% of the price (US$30,000) as a down payment. The financial institution provides the other 80% of the price (US$120,000). This agreement results in 20% of the home ownership belonging to the client and the remaining 80% to the financial institution.

The next step for both parties would be to determine the fair rental value for the property. One way to determine the rental value is for both the client and financial institution to survey the market to obtain estimates for similar properties in the same neighbourhood and negotiate an agreement. This fair rental value will remain constant over the life of the agreement. For this example, we assume US$1000 per month as the rental value.

A rental value of US$1000 means that the client will pay US$800 as rent for the 80% share the financial institution holds. The two parties then agree on the period of financing. In this example we assume that the financing period is 15 years (180 months). Based on the rental value and the financing period, the financial institution then determines the fixed monthly payments the client would have to make to own the house (see Table 6.1).

In this example the client starts by paying US$1147, which includes the required 80% of the US$1000, and extra payment of US$347. By doing so the client reduces the share of the financial institution by US$347, and increases his own share by the same amount. The next month's rental payment of the client would be reduced to US$798, and again the payment made above the rent amount will result in an increase in the client's ownership of the property. This continues on until the client buys back all the shares of the home that the financial institution holds at the end of the agreed financing period.

This simplified example does not take into account fees and payments which the financial institution may charge such as insurance and taxes.

In the event of nonpayment of rent from the client, the financial institution has to take into consideration the reason for the nonpayment. If the client has a valid excuse for nonpayment, the financial institution has to show leniency so that the client does not feel overburdened, and the client should be given more time to make the payment. In theory, if the financial institution charges any extra amount as compensation for the late payment, the amount would be considered as interest and therefore not permitted in Islam. If there is no genuine reason for the late payment, the financial institution can ask the client to make a payment to a charity as a penalty. This prohibition of charging late fees makes it even more important for Islamic financial institutions to evaluate each application carefully before entering into an agreement.

6.1.3   Criticism of *Musharaka*

Musharaka is sometimes criticised as being an old instrument that cannot be applied in the modern world. However, this criticism is unjustified. Islam has not prescribed a specific form or procedure for *Musharaka*, rather it has set some broad principles that can accommodate numerous forms and procedures. A new form or procedure in *Musharaka* that would make it suitable for modern financial needs cannot be rejected merely because it has no precedent in the past. In fact, every new form can be acceptable as long as it conforms to the principles laid down by the *Sharia'a*. Therefore, it is not necessary that *Musharaka* be implemented only in its traditional form.

Another criticism levelled against *Musharaka* is based upon the issue of profits being guaranteed by some financial institutions. Even though *Musharaka* is considered to be the most authentic form of Islamic financing, the risk associated with sharing losses means that it is not as popular as the other modes.

To make the product more appealing to the customer, some financial institutions have started guaranteeing profits in *Musharaka*. By doing so, these institutions are contravening the basic law of Islamic finance that requires linking rewards to risks. If profits are guaranteed, the risk factor is eliminated, making the profit resemble interest. Although these actions may help Islamic banks grow in the short-run, the long-term costs (harm to reputation and authenticity) will outweigh the benefits. Such moves also provide ammunition to the critics of the system, who are already questioning whether the system is nothing more than an interest-based system operating under the guise of profit.

6.2   QUESTIONS

6.2.1   What are the Features of the *Musharaka* Contract?

1. How does *Musharaka* work?

   _____

   _____

   _____

   _____

2. In what sense is *Musharaka* an asset-based or equity-based source of finance?

   _____

   _____

   _____

   _____

3. What is the risk for the *Rab ul Mall* providing the finance?

✎ _____

_____

_____

_____

6.2.2   The *Musharaka* Contract

4. *Musharaka* is an Arabic term which means:
   A. A professional investor.   **T   F**
   B. A joint stock company.   **T   F**
   C. A joint enterprise formed for conducting a business.   **T   F**
5. *Musharaka* is sometimes called:
   A. A silent partnership.   **T   F**
   B. A full partnership.   **T   F**
   C. A limited liability partnership.   **T   F**
6. Profits are shared:
   A. In proportion to the amount invested.   **T   F**
   B. According to a fixed *Sharia'a* ratio.   **T   F**
   C. 50:50.   **T   F**
7. Losses are shared according to:
   A. The proportion of the amount invested.   **T   F**
   B. According to a fixed *Sharia'a* ratio.   **T   F**
   C. 50:50.   **T   F**
8. The difference between *Musharaka* and *Mudaraba* is:
   A. *Musharaka* involves limited liability.   **T   F**
   B. *Mudaraba* involves unlimited liability.   **T   F**
   C. *Musharaka* involves unlimited liability.   **T   F**
9. The difference between *Musharaka* and *Mudaraba* is:
   A. Risks and returns in *Musharaka* are shared in proportion to the capital invested.   **T   F**
   B. Investment in *Mudaraba* comes only from the *Rab ul Mall*.   **T   F**
   C. In *Musharaka* all the partners share the loss in proportion to the ratio of their investment.   **T   F**
   D. In *Mudaraba* any losses are suffered by the *Rab ul Mall* alone.   **T   F**
10. Given the investment split between the *Rab ul Mall* and the partner company illustrated below, indicate the *Sharia'a*-compliant profit and loss share potentially agreed:

	Investment contribution	Profit share agreed	Loss share agreed	
A	40/60	50/50	50/50	T F
B	60/40	70/30	75/25	T F
C	50/50	60/40	60/40	T F
D	75/25	50/50	75/25	T F
E	50/50	60/40	40/60	T F
F	70/30	70/30	60/40	T F
G	60/40	60/40	40/60	T F
H	50/50	70/30	50/50	T F

11. With a diminishing *Musharaka*
    A. The *Rab ul Mall's* share in the equity is reduced each year through repayments made by the borrower.   **T   F**
    B. The borrower buys out the *Rab ul Mall's* share over a period of time.   **T   F**
    C. As the repayment of capital takes place, the *Rab ul Mall* owns a larger share of the asset.   **T   F**

12. Given the investment contribution in a *Musharaka* contract between the *Rab ul Mall* and the partner as outlined below, the following is the *Sharia'a*-compliant profit/loss share that could have been agreed:

Investment contribution	Profit share agreed	Loss share agreed
40/60	50/50	50/50

T   F

13. Given the investment contribution in a *Musharaka* contract between the *Rab ul Mall* and the partner as outlined below, the following is the *Sharia'a*-compliant profit/loss share that could have been agreed:

Investment contribution	Profit share agreed	Loss share agreed
60/40	70/30	75/25

T   F

14. Given the investment contribution in a *Musharaka* contract between the bank as *Rab ul Mall* and the partner, as outlined below, the following is the *Sharia'a*-compliant profit/loss share that could have been agreed:

Investment contribution	Profit share agreed	Loss share agreed
50/50	60/40	60/40

T   F

15. With a *Musharaka* contract, the *Rab ul Mall* has a completely certain rate of return.   **T   F**
16. *Musharaka* is a *Sharia'a*-compliant Islamic mode of finance because the risk is such that if the leased asset is destroyed, without any misuse or negligence on the part of the lessee, it is the *Rab ul Mall* (lessor) who must bear the risk.   **T   F**
17. *Musharaka* is a *Sharia'a*-compliant Islamic mode of finance because the risk is such that if the manufacturer, who has agreed to manufacture the goods, makes faulty goods or does not deliver them on time, the *Rab ul Mall* is at risk.   **T   F**
18. Given the investment contribution, in a *Musharaka* contract, between the *Rab ul Mall* and the partner, outlined below, the following is the *Sharia'a*-compliant profit/loss share that could have been agreed:

Investment contribution	Profit share agreed	Loss share agreed
75/25	50/50	75/25

T   F

19. Given the investment contribution in a *Musharaka* contract between the *Rab ul Mall* and the partner as outlined below, the following is the *Sharia'a*-compliant profit/loss share that could have been agreed:

Investment contribution	Profit share agreed	Loss share agreed
50/50	60/40	40/60

T F

20. With a *Musharaka* contract, the *Rab ul Mall* has a completely uncertain rate of return. **T F**

21. With a *Musharaka* contract, the *Rab ul Mall* has an uncertain rate of return for a short period only. **T F**

22. With a *Musharaka* contract, the cost of capital, for the *Rab ul Mall*, is completely fixed and predetermined. **T F**

23. With a *Musharaka* contract, the cost of capital, for the *Rab ul Mall*, is completely uncertain until the end of the contract. **T F**

24. *Musharaka* is a *Sharia'a*-compliant Islamic mode of finance because the risk is such that, under a profit and loss sharing contract, the *Rab ul Mall* can lose all his capital and the *Mudarib* can lose only the time and effort expended. **T F**

25. *Musharaka* is a *Sharia'a*-compliant Islamic mode of finance because the risk is such that, if the *Rab ul Mall*'s client does not pay on time, or does not pay at all, the *Rab ul Mall* is at risk. **T F**

26. Under a *Musharaka* contract, the *Rab ul Mall* has no control over the management of the funds. **T F**

27. Under a *Musharaka* contract, the *Rab ul Mall* has full control over the management of the funds. **T F**

28. Under a *Musharaka* contract, the *Rab ul Mall* is exposed to a total loss of capital invested. **T F**

29. Under a *Musharaka* contract, the *Rab ul Mall* is exposed to no loss of capital invested. **T F**

30. *Musharaka* is a *Sharia'a*-compliant mode of finance given that the risk is such that if the *Rab ul Mall*'s client, who has been paid upfront, does not deliver the goods at the agreed future date, there is the risk that the *Rab ul Mall* cannot easily resell the goods, exposing itself to risk. **T F**

31. Given the investment contribution in a *Musharaka* contract between the *Rab ul Mall* and the partner as outlined below, the following is the *Sharia'a*-compliant profit/loss share that could have been agreed:

Investment contribution	Profit share agreed	Loss share agreed
70/30	70/30	60/40

T F

32. Given the investment contribution in a *Musharaka* contract between the *Rab ul Mall* and the partner as outlined below, the following is the *Sharia'a*-compliant profit/loss share that could have been agreed:

Investment contribution	Profit share agreed	Loss share agreed
60/40	60/40	40/60

T F

33. Given the investment contribution in a *Musharaka* contract between the bank as *Rab ul Mall* and the partner, outlined below, the following is the *Sharia'a*-compliant profit/loss share that could have been agreed:

Investment contribution	Profit share agreed	Loss share agreed
50/50	70/30	50/50

T F

34. With a diminishing *Musharaka* contract, the *Rab ul Mall*'s share in the equity is reduced each year through repayments made by the borrower. **T F**
35. With a diminishing *Musharaka* contract, the *Rab ul Mall*'s share in the equity is reduced each year through repayments made by the lender. **T F**
36. With a diminishing *Musharaka* contract, the *Rab ul Mall*'s share in the equity is increased each year through repayments made by the borrower. **T F**
37. With a diminishing *Musharaka* contract, as the repayment of capital takes place the *Rab ul Mall* owns a larger share of the asset. **T F**
38. *Musharaka* is a *Sharia'a*-compliant mode of finance because the risk is such that the financial institution and the client, under a profit and loss share contract, have to share the losses in proportion to their respective capital contributions. **T F**
39. With a diminishing *Musharaka* contract, the borrower buys out the *Rab ul Mall*'s share over a period of time. **T F**
40. Under a *Musharaka* contract, the *Rab ul Mall* is at risk for the entire period of the contract. **T F**
41. Under a *Musharaka* contract, the *Rab ul Mall* is at risk for a short period only. **T F**
42. Under a *Musharaka* contract, the *Rab ul Mall* is at risk until the asset completes its life. **T F**
43. Under a *Musharaka* contract, the *Rab ul Mall* is at risk even after the contract has expired. **T F**

For Questions 44 to 46, only one of the potential answers is correct. Insert A, B or C where indicated below each question.

44. Which of the following is the most appropriate definition of *Musharaka*?
    A. *Musharaka* refers to a contract for the sale of an item of property in which the seller declares his cost and adds an agreed profit and sells the item to the buyer at the cost plus an agreed profit.
    B. *Musharaka* refers to a partnership arrangement in which two or more persons contribute capital to an enterprise and one or more of such persons also manage the enterprise.
    C. *Musharaka* refers to a partnership arrangement in which one or more persons contribute funds and one or more persons contribute management effort to an enterprise (but the investors and managers are not the same persons).
    ✎ *Answer:*_____
45. A venture capital firm is willing to participate as an investor in a *Musharaka* financing for a 20-year toll bridge franchise held by a franchise operator. However, the venture capital firm wants to exit in 10 years. Is this permissible?
    A. No, because in *Musharaka* financing the investor must be committed for the entire duration of the venture.

B. Yes, the transaction could be structured as a diminishing *Musharaka* in which the venture capital firm receives extra dividends and the operator's equity share increases over time.

C. Yes, but the venture capital firm and the operator cannot agree to the 10-year term at the time of contracting. The parties could voluntarily agree to a buy-out of the venture capital firm after the financing is implemented.

✎ *Answer:*_____

46. Which of the following statements most accurately depicts the difference or similarity between *Mudaraba* and *Musharaka*?

A. In a *Mudaraba* transaction, the financing party typically does not play a role in management. In a *Musharaka* transaction, the financing party may play a role in management.

B. In both *Mudaraba* and *Musharaka* transactions, the financing party typically plays a role in management.

C. In a *Musharaka* transaction, the financing party typically does not play a role in management. In a *Mudaraba* transaction, the financing party may play a role in management.

✎ *Answer:*_____

6.2.3   Risks with the *Musharaka* Contract

Describe at least two risks associated with the *Musharaka* contract:

Risk 1

✎ _____

_____

_____

_____

_____

_____

Risk 2

✎ _____

_____

_____

_____

_____

_____

6.3   ANSWERS

6.3.1   What are the Features of the *Musharaka* Contract?

1. How does it work?

    The bank forms a partnership with another party. Both partners contribute capital. Profits are allocated according to an agreed proportion while allowing for managerial skills to be remunerated.

2. Money has no intrinsic utility in Islam; it is only a medium of exchange. Making money from money is *riba* and thereby *haram*. Financing in Islam must be asset based or equity based. As it says in the *Qur'an*: 'Allah has permitted trade and prohibited *riba*'.

    The partnership will use the funds for the purchase of real assets which result in productive investment and the creation of wealth. It is thus both equity and asset based.

3. Islam requires that any *Rab ul Mall* profits are only justified if there is risk preference by investors. This is based on the Arabic term *Al Ghunm bil-Ghurm*, i.e., profits must be linked with the investors' willingness to take risk.

    Losses are shared strictly in relation to the respective capital contribution.

6.3.2   The *Musharaka* Contract

4. A. FALSE
   B. FALSE
   C. TRUE
5. A. FALSE
   B. TRUE
   C. FALSE
6. A. FALSE
   B. FALSE
   C. FALSE
7. A. TRUE
   B. TRUE
   C. FALSE
8. A. FALSE
   B. FALSE
   C. TRUE
9. A. TRUE
   B. TRUE
   C. TRUE
   D. TRUE
10. A. FALSE
    B. FALSE
    C. FALSE
    D. TRUE
    E. FALSE
    F. FALSE
    G. FALSE
    H. TRUE

11. A. TRUE
    B. TRUE
    C. FALSE
12. FALSE
13. FALSE
14. FALSE
15. FALSE
16. FALSE
17. FALSE
18. TRUE
19. FALSE
20. TRUE
21. FALSE
22. FALSE
23. TRUE
24. FALSE
25. FALSE
26. FALSE
27. TRUE
28. TRUE
29. FALSE
30. FALSE
31. FALSE
32. FALSE
33. TRUE
34. TRUE
35. FALSE
36. FALSE
37. FALSE
38. TRUE
39. TRUE
40. TRUE
41. FALSE
42. TRUE
43. FALSE
44. B
45. B
46. A

6.3.3   Risks with the *Musharaka* Contract

Describe at least two risks associated with the *Musharaka* contract:

Risk 1 *Credit Risk*: The risk that the entrepreneur/partner defaults and goes bankrupt.
Risk 2 *Operational Risk*: The risk that the partner lacks technical expertise and the project fails.

7
The *Ijara* Contract as a Mode of Islamic Finance

7.1 LEARNING OUTCOMES, SUMMARY OVERVIEW AND PROBLEMS

7.1.1 Learning Outcomes

After reading Chapter 7 you should be able to do the following:

- Define *Ijara*.
- Define *Ijara wa Iqtina* (also known as *Ijara Muntahia Bittamleek*).
- Distinguish a conventional loan from an *Ijara* contract.
- Describe the elements of an *Ijara* transaction.
- Contrast *Ijara* with the other modes of Islamic finance.
- Identify the reasoning behind the *Sharia'a* rulings on *Ijara*.
- Describe the different forms of *Ijara*.
- Explain the practicalities of implementing *Ijara*.
- Identify the Arabic terminology used in *Ijara*.
- Describe the *Sharia'a* rulings on *Ijara*.
- Contrast conventional leasing with Islamic leasing.
- Explain the role that interest can play within an *Ijara* transaction.
- Identify problems associated with applying *Ijara*.
- Explain the importance of deferred sales within Islamic finance.
- Contrast the role of penalty defaults within conventional and Islamic finance.
- Explain how *Ijara* can be used for home finance.
- Define LIBOR and explain its application with an *Ijara* contract.
- Identify the deferred sale versus profit and loss share contracts.
- Test that you have fully understood the principles that underlie the *Ijara* contract.

7.1.2 Summary Overview

The literal meaning of *Ijara* is 'to give something on rent'. As per Islamic jurisprudence the term connotes two distinct situations:

- The services of human beings for wages – the *mustajir* (employer) employing the services of an *ajir* (employee) on wages (*ujrah*) in lieu of hired services. An *ajir* for this purpose can be anyone rendering services including plumbers, doctors and lawyers.
- Usufructs of assets and properties for rent – transferring the usufruct of an asset by *mujir* (lessor) to *mustajir* (lessee) in lieu of *ujrah* (rent) payable by the latter.

To help clarify the processes, *Ijara* and *Ijara wa Iqtina* are depicted as flow charts in Figures 7.1 and 7.2.

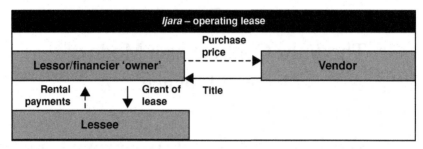

Figure 7.1 *Ijara* – operating lease

Ijara is an Islamic form of leasing. In fact it is another form of mark-up structure. Here the bank buys capital equipment or property and leases it out under instalment plans to end users. As in conventional leasing there may be an option to buy the goods at the end of the *Ijara* built into the contracts. This would be an *Ijara wa Iqtina* contract. The instalments consist of rental for use and part repayment of capital.

The customer selects the asset to be financed and the bank then purchases it from the supplier and leases it to the customer for an agreed period. Refinancing of assets owned by the client, in a sale and leaseback arrangement, is allowed under certain circumstances. The bank, as the owner of the asset, is paid rent, fixed or variable as agreed by the parties. The rental amount is often linked to LIBOR.

The bank must exercise all the lessor's rights and obligations such as maintenance, insurance and repair. The lessee gets the use of the asset for the period of the lease subject to payment of rent. The lessee may assume the obligations such as maintenance for a reduced rent. The fact that there is a real tangible good to be financed means that this is the most *Sharia'a*-compliant of the mark-up products.

Ijara is in high demand and perhaps on its way to becoming the most popular of Islamic financial instruments. It provides the appropriate Islamic financial approach for intermediate- or long-term financing of assets. *Sharia'a* rules permit the levy of rental in lieu of granting the right to use real assets. As the financier undertakes the risk of the ownership he is entitled to receive a return by way of rental under the *Sharia'a*. Normally the rent is fixed so that the financial institution gets back its original investment plus a profit. Finance leases or *Ijara wa Iqtina* embodies an option to purchase the asset at the end of the period.

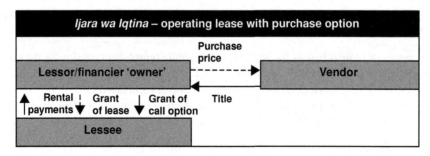

Figure 7.2 *Ijara wa Iqtina* – operating lease with purchase option

7.1.2.1   Comparison with the Conventional Lease

Financial Accounting Standard (FAS) 8, formulated by the Accounting & Auditing Organisation for Islamic Financial Institutions (AAOIFI), provides for accounting treatment for *Ijara* and *Ijara wa Iqtina*. This AAOIFI recommended Standard for *Ijara* and the Standard formulated by International Accounting Standard 17 (IAS 17) for conventional leasing differ in many aspects.

As per IAS 17, a 'lease' is an agreement whereby the lessor conveys to the lessee, in return for a payment or series of payments, the right to use an asset for an agreed period of time. According to IAS 17 a lease is classified as a finance lease if it 'transfers substantially the risks and rewards incidental to ownership'. A lease is classified as an operating lease if it does not transfer substantially all risks and rewards incidental to ownership.

In comparison, FAS 8 defines *Ijara* as 'ownership of the right to the benefit of using an asset in return for consideration' but also embodies the additional condition that the benefit should be *Sharia'a* complaint. Thus *Ijara* and a conventional lease differ regarding the requirement to comply with *Sharia'a*.

Sharia'a does not permit *Ijara* to be used for an asset where *riba* (interest) is involved, one involving merchandise considered as *haram* or for unlawful transactions.

AAOIFI FAS 8 also embodies a classification of *Ijara* into two categories. If the contract refers to a promise to the effect that the legal title would ultimately pass on to the *mustajir* (lessee) at the expiry, it is referred to as *Ijara wa Iqtina*. In this case, which is loosely considered as equivalent to the conventional finance lease, at the expiry of the term the passing of the legal title to the *mustajir* could occur:

- on transfer on payment of balance rentals;
- as a gift;
- on payment of a token or for an amount specified in the contract; or
- on the gradual transfer of the title.

As per AAOIFI Juristic Rules on the fulfilment of a promise, for the transfer to be effective, a contract distinct from the *Ijara* contract should be executed. The *mustajir* has an option, which he may or may not exercise. Thus *Ijara wa Iqtina* would have the characteristics or the substance of a conventional lease only if the *mustajir* exercises the option. In the absence of such exercise, *Ijara wa Iqtina* for all intents and purposes is an operating lease. Hence in legal form and in concept, *Ijara wa Iqtina* and a conventional finance lease are not identical.

Perhaps the key distinction between the *Ijara wa Iqtina* and the conventional finance lease is that in the Islamic version the lessor (*mujir*) undertakes full ownership risks of the corpus of the leased asset. Whereas in the Islamic version the risk remains with the *mujir*, the passing of the risk to the lessee is a prerequisite for a lease to be classified as a finance lease under International Accounting Standards.

With *Ijara*, the risk must follow the legal title unless any damage is caused by the negligence or the misconduct of the *mustajir*. As IAS 17 looks at substance over form for accounting purposes, on the passing of the risks and rewards of the asset to the lessee, the asset is recorded in the books of the lessee coupled with the right to claim depreciation. Major repairs, maintenance and insurance remain to the account of the *mujir* (lessor) in an *Ijara*, whereas these costs are passed on to the lessee in a conventional lease.

7.1.2.2 What if the Asset becomes Faulty?

The comparison of *Ijara* is made clearer over its conventional counterpart when it concerns the asset being faulty due to major defects. During the period in which the asset is out of order, *Ijara* rentals would be suspended so that the *mustajir* (lessee), who cannot benefit from the use of the asset, is provided with financial relief. *Sharia'a* also prohibits the levy of a penalty in an *Ijara* arrangement for delayed payments, unlike in a conventional lease.

The issue of delayed payments may be addressed in an *Ijara* contract by various means such as inclusion of a donation clause, by acceleration of instalments or by the cancellation of the contract. The compassionate attitude towards charging *ujrah* (rent) from the *mustajir* is manifested at the commencement of the charge itself. In a conventional lease the payment obligation may commence from the date of execution of the contract for funding. But in *Ijara* the obligation for the payment commences only upon the delivery of the asset to the *mustajir* or upon enabling the use thereof by him.

7.1.2.3 Structuring Using the Ijara Contract

The apparently simple and straightforward *Ijara* contract can be adopted in order to achieve many ends. An *Ijara* could be the retail structure of a *Sukuk-Al-Ijara*, which permits the originator to raise funds as well as *sukuk* (Islamic bond) holders to trade in the *sukuk* certificates to enable the liquidity management. *Ijara* is also a means for unlocking and realising the capital value of an asset to fulfil the working capital needs of an organisation. A company that already owns an asset may sell it to the financier for immediate funds and continue to use it under an *Ijara* agreement on payment of periodical rentals.

Ijara contracts may be entered into for the long, medium or short term and may be adapted to fulfil the functions of either conventional finance or operating leases. Moreover, these contracts can be subject to English or New York law in international transactions.

7.2 QUESTIONS

7.2.1 What are the Features of the *Ijara* Contract?

1. How does *Ijara* work?

   ✎ _____

   _____

   _____

   _____

2. In what sense is *Ijara* an asset-based or equity-based source of finance?

   ✎ _____

   _____

   _____

   _____

3. What is the risk for the *Rab ul Mall* providing the finance?

✎ _____

_____

_____

_____

7.2.2   The *Ijara* Contract

4. *Ijara* is an Arabic term which means:
   A. To invest in the property market.   **T   F**
   B. To give something to rent.   **T   F**
   C. To help investors seeking to build mosques.   **T   F**
5. The term usufruct, used in *Ijara* contracts, means:
   A. The right to enjoy an asset that is owned by someone else.   **T   F**
   B. To gain the benefits, profit, utility and advantage of using an asset.   **T   F**
   C. While using an asset, to guarantee not to alter the substance of the asset.   **T   F**
6. The lessor is:
   A. The entrepreneur needing funds.   **T   F**
   B. The *Rab ul Mall*.   **T   F**
   C. The *Wakil*.   **T   F**
7. The lessee is:
   A. The *Wakil*.   **T   F**
   B. The borrower.   **T   F**
   C. The *Rab ul Mall*.   **T   F**
8. The basic rules of *Ijara* are:
   A. The owner of an asset transfers its usufruct to another person for an agreed period at an agreed consideration.   **T   F**
   B. The subject of the lease must have a valuable use.   **T   F**
   C. A valid lease must ensure that the corpus of the leased property remains in the ownership of the seller and only its usufruct is transferred to the lessee.   **T   F**
9. Under *Ijara*, the insurance and maintenance is:
   A. Paid by the lessor.   **T   F**
   B. Paid by the lessee.   **T   F**
   C. Normally covered by *Takaful* provided by the lessor.   **T   F**
   D. Normally covered by *Takaful* provided by the lessee.   **T   F**
10. *Ijara* is:
    A. A contract between the lessor and lessee for the use of a specific asset.   **T   F**
    B. A contract whereby the lessor retains ownership of the asset and the lessee has possession and use of the asset.   **T   F**
    C. A contract whereby the lessee pays rent.   **T   F**
11. At the end of the lease period:
    A. The lessee is offered the option of buying the property at a pre-agreed price.   **T   F**
    B. The lessee may be offered the option of buying the property at a price negotiated at the time.   **T   F**

    C. The lessee is not automatically offered the option of buying the property at a price negotiated at that time. **T F**

12. *Ijara* is *Sharia'a* compliant because:
    A. Rental payments provide fixed returns to the *Rab ul Mall.* **T   F**
    B. Rental payments are invested in *Sharia'a*-compliant accounts. **T   F**
    C. Rental payments should be calculated according to the *Sharia'a*, in line with the expected profitability of the venture. **T F**

13. The risk of capital loss with *Ijara* is normally:
    A. Borne by the lessor. **T   F**
    B. Borne by the lessee. **T   F**
    C. Covered by *Takaful* normally provided by the lessor. **T   F**
    D. Covered by *Takaful* normally provided by the lessee. **T   F**

7.2.3   The *Ijara wa Iqtina* Contract

14. Under *Ijara wa Iqtina*, the lessor is:
    A. The entrepreneur needing funds. **T   F**
    B. The *Rab ul Mall.* **T   F**
    C. The *Wakil.* **T   F**

15. Under *Ijara wa Iqtina*, the lessee is:
    A. The *Wakil.* **T   F**
    B. The entrepreneur needing funds. **T   F**
    C. The *Rab ul Mall.* **T   F**

16. Under *Ijara wa Iqtina*, at the end of the lease period:
    A. The lessee is offered the option of buying the property at a pre-agreed price. **T   F**
    B. The lessee is offered the option of buying the property at a price negotiated at that time. **T F**
    C. The lessee is not automatically offered the option of buying the property at a pre-agreed price. **T F**

17. Under *Ijara wa Iqtina*, the lessor:
    A. Is responsible for the maintenance and insurance of the asset. **T   F**
    B. Is not responsible for the maintenance and insurance of the asset. **T   F**
    C. Insists that the lessee pays the *Takaful* costs directly. **T   F**

18. The risk of loss with *Ijara wa Iqtina* is:
    A. Borne by the lessor. **T   F**
    B. Borne by the lessee. **T   F**
    C. Normally covered by *Takaful.* **T   F**

19. Under *Ijara wa Iqtina*, insurance is:
    A. Paid by the lessor. **T   F**
    B. Paid by the lessee. **T   F**
    C. Normally covered by *Takaful* provided by the lessor. **T   F**
    D. Normally covered by *Takaful* provided by the lessee. **T   F**

7.2.4   The *Ijara* Contract in more detail

20. *Ijara* is an Arabic term which means a 'deferred credit sale'. **T   F**
21. *Ijara* is an Arabic term which means to 'give something to rent'. **T   F**

22. The term 'usufruct', used with an *Ijara* contract, means the right to enjoy property that you already own.   **T   F**
23. The term 'usufruct', used with an *Ijara* contract, means the right to enjoy property that is owned by someone else.   **T   F**
24. The term 'usufruct', used with an *Ijara* contract, means that, while using an asset, you guarantee to alter the substance of the asset.   **T   F**
25. The term 'usufruct', used with an *Ijara* contract, means that, while using an asset you guarantee not to alter the substance of the asset.   **T   F**
26. Under an *Ijara* contract, the lessor is the entrepreneur needing funds.   **T   F**
27. Under an *Ijara* contract, the lessor is the *Rab ul Mall*.   **T   F**
28. Under an *Ijara* contract, the lessee is the borrower.   **T   F**
29. Under an *Ijara* contract, the lessee is the *Rab ul Mall*.   **T   F**
30. Under an *Ijara* contract, the insurance and the major maintenance expenses are paid insured by the lessor.   **T   F**
31. Under an *Ijara* contract, the insurance and the major maintenance expenses are paid insured by the lessee.   **T   F**
32. Under an *Ijara* contract, the insurance may be covered by *Takaful*.   **T   F**
33. Under an *Ijara* contract, the insurance cannot be covered by *Takaful*.   **T   F**
34. Under an *Ijara* contract, there is a contract between the lessor and lessee for the use of a specific asset.   **T   F**
35. Under an *Ijara* contract, the lessee retains ownership of the asset and the lessor has possession and use of the asset.   **T   F**
36. Under an *Ijara* contract, the lessor retains ownership of the asset and the lessee has possession and use of the asset.   **T   F**
37. Under an *Ijara* contract, the lessor pays rent.   **T   F**
38. Under an *Ijara* contract, the lessee pays rent.   **T   F**
39. With an *Ijara* contract, at the end of the lease period, the lessee is automatically offered the option of buying the asset.   **T   F**
40. With an *Ijara* contract, at the end of the lease period, the lessee may be offered the option of buying the asset.   **T   F**
41. The *Ijara* contract is *Sharia'a* compliant because rental payments provide fixed returns to the *Rab ul Mall*.   **T   F**
42. The *Ijara* contract is *Sharia'a* compliant because rental payments should ideally be calculated according to the expected profitability of the venture.   **T   F**
43. Under an *Ijara* contract, the risk of capital loss is borne by the lessor.   **T   F**
44. Under an *Ijara* contract, the risk of capital loss is borne by the lessee.   **T   F**
45. Under an *Ijara* contract, the risk of capital loss is normally borne by *Takaful*.   **T   F**
46. Under an *Ijara* contract, the *Rab ul Mall* is at risk until the asset completes its life.   **T   F**
47. Under an *Ijara* contract, the *Rab ul Mall* is at risk even after the contract has expired.   **T   F**
48. Under an *Ijara* contract, the *Rab ul Mall* is exposed to no loss of capital.   **T   F**
49. *Ijara* is a *Sharia'a*-compliant Islamic mode of finance because the risk is such that if the *Rab ul Mall*'s client does not pay on time, or does not pay at all, the *Rab ul Mall* is at risk.   **T   F**
50. *Ijara* is a *Sharia'a*-compliant Islamic mode of finance because the risk is such that the *Rab ul Mall* can lose all his capital and the *Mudarib* can lose only his time and effort expended.   **T   F**

51. *Ijara* is a *Sharia'a*-compliant Islamic mode of finance because the risk is such that the financial institution and the client have to share the losses in proportion to the respective capital contributions. **T F**

52. *Ijara* is a *Sharia'a*-compliant Islamic mode of finance because the risk is such that if the leased asset is destroyed, without any misuse or negligence on the part of the lessee, it is the *Rab ul Mall* (lessor) who must bear the risk. **T F**

53. Under *Ijara wa Iqtina*, insurance can be covered by *Takaful*. **T F**

54. The risk of loss with an *Ijara wa Iqtina* contract can be borne by *Takaful*. **T F**

55. With an *Ijara* contract, the *Rab ul Mall* has a completely certain rate of return. **T F**

56. With an *Ijara* contract, the *Rab ul Mall* has a completely uncertain rate of return. **T F**

57. With an *Ijara* contract, the *Rab ul Mall* has an uncertain rate of return for a short period only. **T F**

58. With an *Ijara* contract, the cost of capital, for the *Rab ul Mall*, is completely fixed and predetermined. **T F**

59. With an *Ijara* contract, the cost of capital, for the *Rab ul Mall*, is completely uncertain until the end of the contract. **T F**

60. *Ijara* is a *Sharia'a*-compliant Islamic mode of finance because the risk is such that if the manufacturer, who has agreed to manufacture the goods, makes faulty goods or does not deliver them on time, the *Rab ul Mall* is at risk. **T F**

61. Under an *Ijara wa Iqtina* contract, at the end of the lease period, the lessee may be offered the option of buying the property at a price negotiated at the beginning of the lease contract. **T F**

62. Under an *Ijara wa Iqtina* contract, at the end of the lease period, the lessee is not automatically offered the option of buying the property at a price agreed at the beginning of the lease contract. **T F**

63. *Ijara* is a *Sharia'a*-compliant Islamic mode of finance because the risk is such that if the *Rab ul Mall*'s client, who has been paid upfront, does not deliver the goods at the agreed future date, there is the risk that the *Rab ul Mall* cannot easily resell the goods, exposing itself to risk. **T F**

64. Under an *Ijara wa Iqtina* contract, the lessor is the entrepreneur needing funds. **T F**

65. Under an *Ijara wa Iqtina* contract, the lessor is the party who owns the assets. **T F**

66. Under an *Ijara wa Iqtina* contract, the lessor is responsible for the major maintenance and for the *Takaful*. **T F**

67. Under an *Ijara wa Iqtina* contract, the lessor is not responsible for the major maintenance and the *Takaful*. **T F**

68. Under an *Ijara wa Iqtina* contract, the lessor will usually insist that the lessee pays the *Takaful* costs directly. **T F**

69. The risk of loss with an *Ijara wa Iqtina* contract is borne by the lessor. **T F**

70. Under an *Ijara wa Iqtina* contract, the lessee is the bank financing the asset. **T F**

71. Under an *Ijara wa Iqtina* contract, at the end of the lease period, the lessee is offered the option of buying the property at a price agreed at the end of the lease contract. **T F**

72. Under an *Ijara* contract, the *Rab ul Mall* has no control over the management of the funds. **T F**

73. Under an *Ijara* contract, the *Rab ul Mall* has full control over the management of the funds. **T F**

74. Under an *Ijara wa Iqtina* contract, insurance is usually paid by the lessor. **T F**

75. Under an *Ijara wa Iqtina* contract, insurance is usually paid by the lessee. **T F**

76. Under an *Ijara wa Iqtina* contract, the lessee is the party using the asset. **T F**
77. Under an *Ijara* contract, the *Rab ul Mall* is exposed to a total loss of funds. **T F**
78. Under an *Ijara* contract, the *Rab ul Mall* is at risk for the entire period of the contract. **T F**
79. Under an *Ijara* contract, the *Rab ul Mall* is at risk for a short period only. **T F**

    For Questions 80 to 83, only one of the potential answers is correct. Insert A, B or C where indicated below each question.

80. Which of the following is the most appropriate definition of *Ijara*?

A. *Ijara* is a form of lease contract in which the owner of a capital asset leases an item to a lessee. The lessee makes specified lease payments over a specified period of time, during which time title to the item of property remains with the owner of the property.

B. *Ijara* is a form of sale contract in which the seller sells and transfers title to an item of property to the buyer at the time of contracting. The buyer pays for the item in instalments.

C. *Ijara* is a form of lease contract for property (land) in which the owner of the property leases a property to a lessee. The lessee makes specified lease payments over a specified period of time, during which time title to the property remains with the owner.

*Answer:*_____

81. A mine operating company approaches an Islamic financial firm to obtain lease financing for some large and quite unique equipment. The financial firm is concerned it will not be able to sell the equipment at the end of the lease term. What form of financing should it propose?

A. The firm should not provide any kind of lease financing because it may not be able to resell the equipment. This type of risk (referred to as residual value risk) cannot be passed on in Islamic financing transactions.

B. The firm should use an *Ijara* contract because, in this type of financing, it can lease the equipment to the company and commit the company to purchase the equipment at the end of the lease term.

C. The firm should use an *Ijara wa Iqtina* contract because, in this type of financing, it can lease the equipment to the company and commit the company to purchasing the equipment at the end of the lease term.

*Answer:*_____

82. Which of the following is the most appropriate definition of *Ijara wa Iqtina*?

A. *Ijara wa Iqtina* is a form of lease contract in which the owner of an item of property leases the item to a lessee. The lessee makes specified lease payments over a specified period of time and has an option to purchase the item at the end of the lease term.

B. *Ijara wa Iqtina* is a form of lease contract in which the owner of an item of property leases the item to a lessee. The lessee makes specified lease payments over a specified period of time and also makes a commitment to purchase the item at the end of the lease term.

C. *Ijara wa Iqtina* is a form of lease contract in which the owner of an item of property leases the item to a lessee. The lessee makes specified lease payments over a specified period of time but does not have an option commitment to purchase the item at the end of the lease term.

*Answer:*_____

7.2.5   Risks with the *Ijara* Contract

Describe at least two risks associated with the *Ijara* contract:

Risk 1

✎ _____

_____

_____

_____

_____

_____

Risk 2

✎ _____

_____

_____

_____

_____

7.3   ANSWERS

7.3.1   What are the Features of the *Ijara* Contract?

1. How does *Ijara* work?

    The bank buys the asset from the vendor. It leases the asset to the lessee in exchange for the usufruct, the right to use the profits of something belonging to another. The lessor receives rental payments.

2. In what sense is *Ijara* an asset-based or equity-based source of finance?

    Money has no intrinsic utility in Islam; it is only a medium of exchange. Making money from money is *riba* and thereby *haram*. Financing in Islam must be asset or equity based. As it says in the *Qur'an*: 'Allah has permitted trade and prohibited *riba*'.

    Ijara is used for tangible assets, buildings, vehicles and so on. The banker provides an asset having usufruct, making it asset based.

3. What is the risk for the *Rab ul Mall* providing the finance?

    Any *Rab ul Mall* profit should be generated with an associated risk.

    Islam requires that any profits are only justified if there is risk preference by investors. This is based on the Arabic term *Al Ghunm bil-Ghurm*, i.e., profits must be linked with the investors' willingness to take risk.

    The lessor assumes risk. If the leased asset is destroyed without any misuse or negligence on the part of the lessee, it is the *Rab ul Mall* who suffers.

7.3.2 The *Ijara* Contract

4. A. FALSE
   B. TRUE
   C. FALSE
5. A. TRUE
   B. TRUE
   C. TRUE
6. A. FALSE
   B. TRUE
   C. FALSE
7. A. FALSE
   B. TRUE
   C. FALSE
8. A. TRUE
   B. TRUE
   C. TRUE
9. A. TRUE
   B. FALSE
   C. TRUE
   D. FALSE
10. A. TRUE
    B. TRUE
    C. TRUE
11. A. FALSE
    B. TRUE
    C. TRUE
12. A. FALSE
    B. FALSE
    C. TRUE
13. A. TRUE
    B. FALSE
    C. TRUE
    D. FALSE

7.3.3 The *Ijara Wa Iqtina* Contract

14. A. FALSE
    B. TRUE
    C. FALSE
15. A. FALSE
    B. TRUE
    C. FALSE
16. A. TRUE
    B. FALSE
    C. FALSE
17. A. FALSE

B. TRUE
C. TRUE
18. A. FALSE
B. TRUE
C. TRUE
19. A. FALSE
B. TRUE
C. FALSE
D. TRUE

7.3.4   The *Ijara* Contract in more detail

20. FALSE
21. TRUE
22. FALSE
23. TRUE
24. FALSE
25. TRUE
26. FALSE
27. TRUE
28. TRUE
29. FALSE
30. TRUE
31. FALSE
32. TRUE
33. FALSE
34. TRUE
35. FALSE
36. TRUE
37. FALSE
38. TRUE
39. FALSE
40. TRUE
41. FALSE
42. TRUE
43. TRUE
44. FALSE
45. TRUE
46. TRUE
47. FALSE
48. FALSE
49. FALSE
50. FALSE
51. FALSE
52. TRUE
53. TRUE
54. TRUE

55. FALSE
56. TRUE
57. FALSE
58. TRUE
59. FALSE
60. FALSE
61. TRUE
62. FALSE
63. FALSE
64. FALSE
65. TRUE
66. FALSE
67. TRUE
68. TRUE
69. FALSE
70. FALSE
71. FALSE
72. FALSE
73. TRUE
74. FALSE
75. TRUE
76. TRUE
77. FALSE
78. TRUE
79. FALSE
80. A
81. C
82. B

7.3.5 Risks with the *Ijara* Contract

Risk 1 *Credit Risk*: The risk that the lessee is unable to service the lease rental as and when it is due.

Risk 2 *Market Risk*: The risk that if default occurs, the bank has to re-rent the property on the open market at a lower price than agreed.

The *Istisna'a* Contract as a Mode of Islamic Finance

8.1 LEARNING OUTCOMES, SUMMARY OVERVIEW AND PROBLEMS

8.1.1 Learning Outcomes

After reading Chapter 8 you should be able to do the following:

- Define *Istisna'a*.
- Define Parallel *Istisna'a*.
- Distinguish a conventional loan from an *Istisna'a* contract.
- Identify the Arabic terminology used in an *Istisna'a* contract.
- Describe the elements of an *Istisna'a* transaction.
- Contrast *Istisna'a* with the other modes of Islamic finance.
- Identify the reasoning behind the *Sharia'a* rulings on *Istisna'a*.
- Explain the practicalities of implementing *Istisna'a*.
- Describe the *Sharia'a* rulings on *Istisna'a*.
- Explain the role that interest can play within an *Istisna'a* transaction.
- Identify problems associated with applying *Istisna'a*.
- Explain the importance of deferred sales within Islamic finance.
- Contrast the role of penalty defaults within conventional and Islamic finance.
- Explain how *Istisna'a* can be used for home finance.
- Define LIBOR and explain its application with an *Istisna'a* contract.
- Identify the deferred sale versus profit and loss share contracts.
- Test that you have fully understood the principles that underlie the *Istisna'a* contract.

8.1.2 Summary Overview

Under an *Istisna'a* contract, the financier provides funds to a supplier who agrees to manufacture, construct, assemble or package a specific asset. As a result, the financier acquires title to the asset and immediately sells or leases it back to the supplier.

Istisna'a is a contract of exchange with deferred delivery, applied to specified made-to-order items.

Istisna'a differs from *Ijara* in that the manufacturer must procure his own raw materials. Otherwise the contract would amount to a hiring of the seller's wage labour as occurs under *Ijara*. *Istisna'a* also differs from *Salam* in that in point (a) above, the subject matter of the contract is always a made-to-order item. In addition other differences are that:

- The delivery date need not be fixed in advance.
- Full advance payment is not required.
- The *Istisna'a* contract can be cancelled but only before the seller commences manufacture of the agreed item(s).

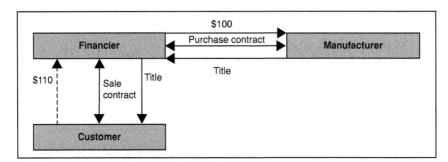

Figure 8.1 *Istisna'a* mode of finance

Figure 8.1 depicts *Istisna'a* as a mode of finance.

Istisna'a is the Islamic vehicle for financing construction or manufacturing projects such as apartment buildings, aircraft, shipbuilding and so on. A significant feature of *Istisna'a* is that it permits a financing transaction to take place in compliance with the *Sharia'a* even though the subject matter of the transaction does not exist at the time of the contract. Another important feature is that payments can either be immediate or deferred.

The steps involved in an *Istisna'a* sale are as follows:

1. The client initiates the process by expressing, to the bank, his desire to manufacture or construct an asset at a specific cost. He gives detailed specifications of the item to be manufactured, constructed or fabricated.
2. The bank agrees to manufacture, construct or fabricate and to deliver the asset to the client in a specific time period.
3. The bank then enters into a contract with the manufacturer, contractor or fabricator, who agrees to manufacture, construct or fabricate the specified asset and deliver it in due time.
4. Final delivery of the asset is made either to the bank, or to the client, as agreed in the contract.
5. Customer payments can be immediate or deferred.

Sharia'a rulings for *Istisna'a* are as follows:

(a) The nature and quality of the item to be delivered must be specified.
(b) The manufacturer must make a commitment to produce the item as described.
(c) The delivery date is not fixed; the item is deliverable upon completion by the manufacturer.
(d) The contract is irrevocable after the commencement of manufacture except where delivered goods do not meet the contracted terms.
(e) Payment can be made in one lump sum or in instalments, and at any time up to or after the time of delivery.
(f) The manufacturer is responsible for the sourcing of inputs to the production process.

An Islamic bank can use *Istisna'a* in two different ways:

• It is permissible for the bank to buy a commodity under an *Istisna'a* contract and sell it either on receipt of a cash instalment or on a deferred payment basis.

- It is also permissible for the bank to enter into *Istisna'a* contract in the capacity of seller to a client who needs to purchase a particular commodity and then draw a Parallel *Istisna'a* contract in the capacity of a buyer with another party to make (manufacture) the commodity agreed upon in the first contract.

The first *Istisna'a* can be immediate or deferred (as regards the payment). The payment terms in the second *Istisna'a* can also be cash or deferred. Contracts in the nature of Build, Operate and Transfer (BOT) can be categorised as *Istisna'a* transactions. For example, a government may enter into a contract with a builder to be repaid through a toll collection over a specified period. *Istisna'a* is also applied in the construction industry including apartment buildings, hospitals, schools and universities.

The practical steps of an *Istisna'a* sale and Parallel *Istisna'a* are as follows:

1. **Istisna'a sale contract:**
   The buyer expresses his desire to buy a commodity and makes an *Istisna'a* request to the bank with a specific price. The timing of payment, whether cash or deferred, shall be subject to agreement.
   The bank usually calculates what it will actually pay in a Parallel *Istisna'a* contract plus the profit it deems reasonable.
   The bank puts itself under an obligation to manufacture a certain commodity and to deliver it in a specific period subject to agreement (the bank puts into consideration whether the due date is the same or after the due date of its receipt to the commodity in the parallel contract).
2. **Parallel *Istisna'a* contract:**
   The bank expresses its desire to order the manufacture of the commodity it has undertaken to manufacture in the first *Istisna'a* contract (with the same specification as in the first contract) and agrees with the manufacturer on the price and the date of delivery.
   The seller puts himself under obligation to manufacture the specific commodity and to its delivery on the agreed due date agreed.
3. **Delivery and receipt of the commodity:**
   The seller delivers the manufactured commodity to the bank directly or to any party at the place decided by the bank on the contract.
   The bank delivers the manufactured commodity directly to the purchaser or authorises any party to deliver the commodity to the purchaser, who has the right to make sure that the commodity satisfies the specification demanded in the contract.

8.2   QUESTIONS

8.2.1   What are the Features of the *Istisna'a* Contract?

1. How does *Istisna'a* work?

✎_____

_____

_____

_____

2. In what sense is *Istisna'a* an asset-based or equity-based source of finance?

   ✎ _____

   _____

   _____

   _____

3. What is the risk for the *Rab ul Mall* providing the finance?

   ✎ _____

   _____

   _____

   _____

8.2.2 The *Istisna'a* Contract

4. *Istisna'a* is an Arabic term which means:
   A. An order to manufacture a specific physical asset for the purchaser.   **T   F**
   B. An agreement to provide working capital for whatever the purchaser needs.   **T   F**
   C. A financing project usually involving the petroleum industry.   **T   F**
5. *Al-mustasni* is an Arabic term which means:
   A. The asset to be built.   **T   F**
   B. The manufacturer of the asset.   **T   F**
   C. The buyer of the asset.   **T   F**
6. *Al-musania'a* is an Arabic term which means:
   A. The manufacturer of the asset.   **T   F**
   B. The asset to be built.   **T   F**
   C. The buyer of the asset.   **T   F**
7. *Al-masnoo* is an Arabic term which means:
   A. The buyer of the asset.   **T   F**
   B. The manufacturer of the asset.   **T   F**
   C. The asset to be built.   **T   F**
8. *Istisna'a* can only be used for:
   A. Syndicated banking projects.   **T   F**
   B. Agricultural projects.   **T   F**
   C. Manufacturing projects.   **T   F**
9. *Istisna'a* involves the following contractual relationships:
   A. *Rab ul Mall* enters into contract with the *al-mustasni*.   **T   F**
   B. *Rab ul Mall* enters into a contract with the *al-musania'a*.   **T   F**
   C. *Rab ul Mall* enters into contract with the *al-masnoo*.   **T   F**
10. Under *Istisna'a*, the *Rab ul Mall*'s role is that of:
   A. Seller of the asset.   **T   F**
   B. Borrower/lender.   **T   F**
   C. Buyer of the asset.   **T   F**

11. The difference between *Istisna'a* and *Murabaha* is:
    A. Under *Murabaha*, the *Rab ul Mall* will buy the goods before they are physically available. **T F**
    B. Under *Murabaha*, the *Rab ul Mall* will buy the goods after they are physically available. **T F**
    C. Under *Istisna'a*, the *Rab ul Mall* will buy the goods before they are constructed. **T F**
    D. Under *Istisna'a*, the *Rab ul Mall* will buy the goods after they are constructed. **T F**
12. The difference between *Istisna'a* and *Salam* is:
    A. *Istisna'a* refers to something needing manufacturing whereas *Salam* does not. **T F**
    B. Under *Salam*, the price must be paid in full in advance unlike *Istisna'a*. **T F**
    C. Under *Istisna'a*, the price must be paid in full in advance unlike *Salam*. **T F**
13. Under the *Sharia'a*, the following applies:
    A. It is normally forbidden to sell something that does not currently exist. **T F**
    B. A seller must normally have acquired ownership of the asset before he can sell it. **T F**
    C. Under *Salam*, agricultural goods are sold before they are grown and therefore they are not *Sharia'a* compliant. **T F**
    D. Under *Istisna'a*, goods are sold before they are manufactured and therefore they are not *Sharia'a* compliant. **T F**
14. Under an *Istisna'a* contract, *al-musania'a* is the asset that must be built. **T F**
15. *Istisna'a* is a *Sharia'a*-compliant Islamic mode of finance because the risk is such that if the bank's client does not pay on time, or does not pay at all, the *Rab ul Mall* is at risk. **T F**
16. *Istisna'a* is a *Sharia'a*-compliant Islamic mode of finance because the risk is such that the *Rab ul Mall* can lose all his capital and the *Mudarib* can lose only his time and effort expended. **T F**
17. *Istisna'a* is a *Sharia'a*-compliant Islamic mode of finance because the risk is such that the financial institution and the client have to share the losses in proportion to the respective capital contributions. **T F**
18. Under an *Istisna'a* contract, *al-musania'a* means the buyer of the asset. **T F**
19. Under an *Istisna'a* contract, *al-musania'a* means the asset that must be built. **T F**
20. Under an *Istisna'a* contract, *al-masnoo'* means the manufacturer of the asset. **T F**
21. Under an *Istisna'a* contract, *al-masnoo* means the asset to be built. **T F**
22. *Istisna'a* is a *Sharia'a*-compliant mode of finance given that the risk is such that if the leased asset is destroyed, without any misuse or negligence on the part of the lessee, it is the *Rab ul Mall* (lessor) who must bear the risk. **T F**
23. *Istisna'a* is a *Sharia'a*-compliant mode of finance given that the risk is such that if the *Rab ul Mall*'s client, who has been paid upfront, does not deliver the goods at the agreed future date, there is the risk that the *Rab ul Mall* cannot easily resell the goods, exposing himself to risk. **T F**
24. Under an *Istisna'a* contract, *al-musania'a* means the manufacturer of the asset. **T F**
25. *Istisna'a* is a *Sharia'a*-compliant mode of finance because the risk is such that if the manufacturer, who has agreed to manufacture the goods, makes faulty goods or does not deliver them on time, the *Rab ul Mall* is at risk. **T F**
26. Under an *Istisna'a* contract, *al-mustasni* means the buyer of the asset. **T F**
27. Under an *Istisna'a* contract, *al-mustasni* means the manufacturer of the asset. **T F**
28. Under an *Istisna'a* contract, *al-masnoo* means the buyer of the asset. **T F**

8.2.3 *Istisna'a* and *Salam* Contracts

29. *Istisna'a* is an Arabic term that means a 'deferred credit sale'.   **T   F**
30. *Istisna'a* is an Arabic term that means 'an order to manufacture a specific physical asset for the purchaser'.   **T   F**
31. *Istisna'a* is an Arabic term that means 'an agreement to provide working capital for business'.   **T   F**
32. Under an *Istisna'a* contract, *al-musania'a* means the asset that must be built.   **T   F**
33. Under an *Istisna'a* contract, *al-mustasni* means the manufacturer of the asset.   **T   F**
34. Under an *Istisna'a* contract, *al-mustasni* means the buyer of the asset.   **T   F**
35. *Istisna'a* can only be used for agricultural projects.   **T   F**
36. *Istisna'a* can only be used for manufacturing projects.   **T   F**
37. *Istisna'a* consists of a contract whereby a *Rab ul Mall* enters into a contract with the entrepreneur/buyer.   **T   F**
38. *Istisna'a* consists of a contract whereby a *Rab ul Mall* enters into a contract with the manufacturer/contractor.   **T   F**
39. Under an *Istisna'a* contract, a bank's role is that of *Rab ul Mall*/seller.   **T   F**
40. Under an *Istisna'a* contract, a *Rab ul Mall*'s role is that of borrower/lender.   **T   F**
41. One difference between *Istisna'a* and *Murabaha* is that, with a *Murabaha* contract, a customer can only buy the goods when they are constructed.   **T   F**
42. One difference between *Istisna'a* and *Murabaha* is that, with a *Murabaha* contract, a customer can buy the goods before they are constructed.   **T   F**
43. One difference between *Istisna'a* and *Murabaha* is that, with an *Istisna'a* contract, the *Rab ul Mall* can buy the goods before they are constructed.   **T   F**
44. One difference between *Istisna'a* and *Salam* is that an *Istisna'a* contract refers to something needing manufacturing whereas a *Salam* contract does not.   **T   F**
45. One difference between *Istisna'a* and *Salam* is that under a *Salam* contract the full price is paid to the deliverer of the goods in advance.   **T   F**
46. Under a *Salam* contract agricultural goods are sold before they are grown, therefore they are not *Sharia'a* compliant.   **T   F**
47. Under a *Salam* contract, a seller must deliver the goods as agreed on the due date.   **T   F**
48. Under a *Salam* contract, a seller assumes full responsibilities for delivery at the agreed price.   **T   F**
49. One of the benefits to a seller of crops, with a *Salam* contract, is that he is not responsible in the event that bad weather destroys his crops.   **T   F**
50. One of the benefits to a seller of crops, with a *Salam* contract, is that he gets paid in advance.   **T   F**
51. One of the benefits to a seller of crops, with a *Salam* contract, is that he can cancel the contract and sell the goods to another buyer if prices have risen meanwhile.   **T   F**
52. Under the *Sharia'a*, one cannot normally sell something that does not currently exist.   **T   F**
53. Under a *Salam* contract, goods are sold before they are grown, and therefore they are not *Sharia'a* compliant.   **T   F**
54. Under an *Istisna'a* contract, goods are sold before they are manufactured, and therefore they are not *Sharia'a* compliant.   **T   F**
55. Which of the following is the most appropriate definition of *Istisna'a*?
    A. *Istisna'a* is a contractual agreement for producing goods and constructing facilities, allowing cash payment in advance and future delivery or a future payment and future delivery.

B. *Istisna'a* is a contractual agreement for producing goods and constructing facilities, allowing cash payment in advance and future delivery. However, it cannot involve a commitment for both a future payment and future delivery.

C. *Istisna'a* refers to an interest-free loan that is made either for charitable purposes or for short-term financing.

✎ *Answer*:_____

8.2.4 Risks with the *Istisna'a* Contract

Describe at least two risks associated with the *Istisna'a* contract:

Risk 1

✎ _____

_____

_____

_____

_____

_____

Risk 2

✎ _____

_____

_____

_____

_____

_____

8.3 ANSWERS

8.3.1 What are the Features of the *Istisna'a* Contract?

1. How does *Istisna'a* work?

   This is a deferred delivery sale. The bank commissions a manufacturer to create the goods needed by the potential buyer. The bank pays for the goods and then charges the buyer.

2. In what sense is *Istisna'a* an asset-based or equity-based source of finance?

   Money has no intrinsic utility in Islam; it is only a medium of exchange. Making money from money is '*riba*' and thereby *haram*. Financing in Islam must be asset or equity based. As it says in the *Qur'an*: 'Allah has permitted trade and prohibited *riba*'.

   The bank has bought real assets which the buyer can use in productive investment, making it asset based.

3. What is the risk for the *Rab ul Mall* providing the finance?

Islam requires that any profits are only justified if there is risk preference by investors. This is based on the Arabic term *Al Ghunm bil-Ghurm* i.e. profits must be linked with the investors' willingness to take risk.

There is the risk that the manufacturer makes faulty goods or does not deliver on time.

8.3.2 The *Istisna'a* Contract

4. A. TRUE
   B. FALSE
   C. FALSE
5. A. FALSE
   B. FALSE
   C. TRUE
6. A. TRUE
   B. FALSE
   C. FALSE
7. A. FALSE
   B. FALSE
   C. TRUE
8. A. FALSE
   B. FALSE
   C. TRUE
9. A. TRUE
   B. TRUE
   C. FALSE
10. A. TRUE
    B. FALSE
    C. TRUE
11. A. FALSE
    B. TRUE
    C. TRUE
    D. FALSE
12. A. TRUE
    B. TRUE
    C. FALSE
13. A. TRUE
    B. TRUE
    C. FALSE
    D. FALSE
14. FALSE
15. FALSE
16. FALSE
17. FALSE
18. FALSE
19. FALSE
20. FALSE

21. TRUE
22. FALSE
23. FALSE
24. TRUE
25. TRUE
26. FALSE
27. FALSE
28. FALSE

8.3.3 *Istisna'a* and *Salam* **Contracts**

29. FALSE
30. TRUE
31. FALSE
32. FALSE
33. FALSE
34. TRUE
35. FALSE
36. TRUE
37. TRUE
38. TRUE
39. TRUE
40. FALSE
41. TRUE
42. FALSE
43. TRUE
44. TRUE
45. TRUE
46. FALSE
47. TRUE
48. TRUE
49. FALSE
50. TRUE
51. FALSE
52. TRUE
53. FALSE
54. FALSE
55. A

8.3.4 **Risks with the *Istisna'a* Contract**

Risk 1 *Credit Risk*: The risk that the customer is unable to honour the payment obligations for deferred instalments when the work is already in progress.

Risk 2 *Operational Risk*: The risk that the partner lacks technical expertise and the project fails.

The *Salam* Contract as a Mode of Islamic Finance

9.1 LEARNING OUTCOMES, SUMMARY OVERVIEW AND PROBLEMS

9.1.1 Learning Outcomes

After reading Chapter 9 you should be able to do the following:

- Define the *Salam* contract.
- Define the Parallel *Salam* contract.
- Distinguish a conventional loan from a *Salam* contract.
- Describe the elements of a *Salam* transaction.
- Contrast *Salam* with the other modes of Islamic finance.
- Identify and understand the Arabic terminology used in *Salam*.
- Identify the reasoning behind the *Sharia'a* rulings on *Salam*.
- Explain the practicalities of implementing *Salam*.
- Describe the *Sharia'a* rulings on *Salam*.
- Explain the role that interest can play within a *Salam* transaction.
- Identify problems with applying *Salam*.
- Describe the different forms of *Salam*.
- Explain the importance of deferred sales within Islamic finance.
- Contrast the role of penalty defaults within conventional and Islamic finance.
- Define LIBOR and explain its application with a *Salam* contract.
- Identify the deferred sale versus profit and loss share contracts.
- Test that you have fully understood the principles that underlie the *Salam* contract.

9.1.2 Summary Overview

The Organisation of Islamic Conference Islamic Fiqh Academy in Jeddah has recognised *Salam* as a *Sharia'a*-compliant mode of Islamic banking.

Salam means a contract in which advance payment is made for goods to be delivered at a later date. The seller undertakes to supply some specific goods to the buyer at a future date in exchange for a price fully paid in advance at the time of contract. It is necessary that the quality of the commodity intended to be purchased is fully specified leaving no ambiguity that may lead to dispute. The objects of this sale are goods and cannot be gold, silver or currencies. Barring the latter examples, *Salam* covers almost anything that is capable of being accurately described as to quantity, quality and workmanship.

It is necessary for the validity of *Salam* that the buyer pays the price in full to the seller at the time of effecting the sale. This is necessary because, in the absence of full payment by the buyer, it will be tantamount to a sale of debt against debt, which is expressly prohibited

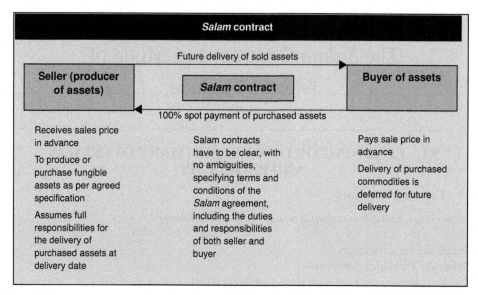

Figure 9.1 *Salam* flow chart

under the *Sharia'a*. Moreover, the basic wisdom behind the permissibility of *Salam* is to fulfil the instant needs of the seller. If the price is not paid to him in full, the basic purpose of the transaction will be defeated.

Salam can be effected only in commodities whose quality and quantity can be specified precisely. Items whose quality or quantity is not determined by the specification cannot be sold through the contract of *Salam*. For example, precious stones cannot be sold on the basis of *Salam*, because each stone is normally different from another in quality, size or weight. Therefore, exact specification is not generally possible.

Figure 9.1 depicts the *Salam* contract as a flow chart.

Salam cannot be used for a particular commodity or on a product of a particular field or farm. For example, if the seller undertakes to supply wheat from a particular field, or the fruit of a particular tree, the *Salam* will not be valid, because there is a possibility that produce of that particular field or the fruit of that tree is destroyed before delivery and, given this possibility, the delivery remains uncertain. The same rule is applicable to every commodity whose supply is not certain.

It is necessary that the quality of the commodity (intended to be purchased through *Salam*) be fully specified leaving no ambiguity that may lead to dispute. All possible details in this respect must be expressly mentioned.

It is also necessary that the quantity of the commodity be agreed upon in unequivocal terms. If the commodity is quantified by weight according to the usage of its traders, its weight must be determined, and if it is quantified through being measured, its exact measure should be known. What is normally weighed cannot be specified by measures and vice versa.

The exact date of delivery must be specified in the contract. *Salam* cannot be effected in respect of those things that must be delivered at spot. For example, if gold is purchased in exchange for silver, it is necessary, according to the *Sharia'a*, that the delivery of both be simultaneous. Here, *Salam* cannot work. Similarly, if wheat is bartered for barley, the simultaneous delivery of both is necessary for the validity of sale. The effect is that the contract of *Salam*, in this case, again is not allowed.

A *Salam* sale is not permissible with existing commodities because damage and deterioration cannot be ruled out before delivery on the due date. Delivery may become impossible. *Salam* is permissible on a commodity of a specific locality if it is assured that it is almost always available in that locality and it rarely becomes unavailable. The place of delivery must be stated in the contract if the commodity needs loading or necessitates transportation expenses.

It is permissible to take a mortgage and guarantor on *Salam* debt to guarantee that the seller satisfies his obligation by delivering the commodity sold, which is a liability on the due date. It is not permissible for the buyer of a *Salam* commodity to sell it before receiving it because that is similar to the prohibited sale of debts. The *Salam* commodity is a liability or debt on the seller and is not an existing commodity.

A *Salam* sale is suitable for the finance of agricultural operations, where the bank can transact with farmers who are expected to have the commodity in plenty during harvest – either from their own crops or the crops of others – which they can buy and deliver in case their own crops fail. Thus the bank renders valuable services to farmers in this way enabling them to achieve their production targets.

A *Salam* sale is also used to finance commercial and industrial activities, especially phases prior to the production and export of commodities. The *Salam* sale is applied by banks in financing craftspeople and small producers by supplying them with inputs of production as *Salam* capital in exchange for some of their commodities to re-market. The scope of *Salam* sale is large enough to cover the needs of various groups such as farmers, industrialists, contractors or traders. It can provide finance for a variety of operational costs and working capital.

9.2 QUESTIONS

9.2.1 What are the Features of the *Salam* Contract

1. How does *Salam* work?

   _____

   _____

   _____

   _____

2. In what sense is *Salam* an asset-based or equity-based source of finance?

   _____

   _____

   _____

   _____

3. What is the risk for the *Rab ul Mall* providing the finance?

   _____

   _____

   _____

   _____

9.2.2 The *Salam* Contract

4. *Salam* is an Arabic term which means:
   A. Purchase/sale of a commodity for immediate delivery in exchange for deferred payment, according to the specified conditions.   **T   F**
   B. Purchase/sale of a commodity for deferred delivery in exchange for immediate payment, according to specified conditions.   **T   F**
   C. Purchase/sale of a commodity for deferred delivery in exchange for deferred payment, according to the specified conditions.   **T   F**
5. Under *Salam*, the seller:
   A. Receives the sale price in advance.   **T   F**
   B. Must deliver the goods as agreed on the due date.   **T   F**
   C. Assumes full responsibility for delivery at the agreed sale price.   **T   F**
6. *Salam* can only be used for:
   A. Project finance.   **T   F**
   B. Manufactured goods.   **T   F**
   C. Agricultural goods.   **T   F**
7. The benefits to the seller with a *Salam* contract are as follows:
   A. He does not need to repay if bad weather destroys his crops.   **T   F**
   B. He gets paid in advance.   **T   F**
   C. He can sell the goods to another buyer if prices have gone up meanwhile.   **T   F**
8. The difference between *Salam* and *Istisna'a* is:
   A. *Istisna'a* refers to something needing manufacturing whereas with *Salam* it does not.   **T   F**
   B. Under *Salam* the price must be paid in full in advance, whereas with *Istisna'a* it does not.   **T   F**
   C. Under *Istisna'a* the price must be paid in full in advance, whereas with *Salam* it does not.   **T   F**
9. Under the *Sharia'a*:
   A. It is normally forbidden to sell something that does not currently exist.   **T   F**
   B. The seller must have acquired ownership of the asset before he can sell it.   **T   F**
   C. *Salam* goods are sold before they exist and are therefore not *Sharia'a*-compliant transactions.   **T   F**
   D. *Istisna'a* assets are sold before they exist and are therefore not *Sharia'a*-compliant transactions.   **T   F**
10. With a *Salam* contract the *muslam fihi* refers to:
    A. The purchaser of the goods.   **T   F**
    B. The commodity to be delivered.   **T   F**
    C. The seller of the goods.   **T   F**
11. With a *Salam* contract the *muslam ileihi* refers to:
    A. The purchaser of the goods.   **T   F**
    B. The commodity to be delivered.   **T   F**
    C. The seller of the goods.   **T   F**
12. With a *Salam* contract the *muslam* refers to:
    A. The purchaser of the goods.   **T   F**
    B. The commodity to be delivered.   **T   F**
    C. The seller of the goods.   **T   F**

13. Under a *Salam* contract the *Rab ul Mall* is at risk for the entire period of the contract.   **T   F**
14. Under a *Salam* contract the *Rab ul Mall* is at risk for a short period only.   **T   F**
15. Under a *Salam* contract the *Rab ul Mall* is at risk until the *muslam ileihi* buys the goods.   **T   F**
16. Under a *Salam* contract the *Rab ul Mall* is at risk even after the contract has expired.   **T   F**
17. Under a *Salam* contract the *Rab ul Mall* is exposed to a total loss of capital.   **T   F**
18. Under a *Salam* contract the *Rab ul Mall* is exposed to no loss of capital.   **T   F**
19. *Salam* is a *Sharia'a*-compliant Islamic mode of finance because the risk is such that the *Rab ul Mall* can lose all his capital and the *Mudarib* can lose only his time and effort expended.   **T   F**
20. *Salam* represents a type of options contract.   **T   F**
21. *Salam* represents a type of forward contract.   **T   F**
22. The concept of *Salam* refers to a sale whereby the seller undertakes to supply a specific commodity to the buyer, at a future date, in return for an advance payment, paid in full in the future.   **T   F**
23. The concept of *Salam* refers to a sale whereby the buyer undertakes to supply a specific commodity to the seller, at a future date, in return for an advance payment, paid in full in the future.   **T   F**
24. The concept of *Salam* refers to a sale whereby the seller undertakes to supply a specific commodity to the buyer, at a future date, in return for an payment, paid in full immediately (spot).   **T   F**
25. The price in *Salam* is spot cash but the supply of the goods is deferred.   **T   F**
26. The incentive for the buyer of a *Salam* contract is that the advance payment is usually more than the amount that would have to be paid if the buyer deferred his purchase and bought the same commodity spot in the future.   **T   F**
27. The incentive for the buyer of a *Salam* contract is that the advance payment may be less than the amount that would have to be paid if the buyer deferred his purchase and bought the same commodity spot in the future.   **T   F**
28. Forward contracts are mostly forbidden under *Sharia'a* law, due to *gharar*.   **T   F**
29. *Salam* is a *Sharia'a*-compliant Islamic mode of finance because the risk is such that if the *Rab ul Mall*'s client, who has been paid upfront, does not deliver the goods at the agreed future date, there is the risk that the *Rab ul Mall* cannot easily resell the goods, exposing himself to risk.   **T   F**
30. Forward contracts are mostly forbidden under *Sharia'a* law, due to *Takaful*.   **T   F**
31. Forward contracts are sometimes permitted under *Sharia'a* law, although strict conditions are attached.   **T   F**
32. With a *Salam* contract the initial payment by the buyer must be paid in full, to ensure that there is no uncertainty over the outstanding payments.   **T   F**
33. *Salam* can only be used for commodities that are standardised, and where the quality can be measured exactly.   **T   F**
34. *Salam* can be used for commodities that are non-standardised, and where the quality is well known.   **T   F**
35. One of the *Sharia'a* conditions, necessary for a *Salam* contract, is that full payment must be made by the seller at the time of effecting the sale.   **T   F**
36. One of the *Sharia'a* conditions, necessary for a *Salam* contract, is that the underlying asset should be an item that is to be produced or purchased by the seller.   **T   F**

37. One of the *Sharia'a* conditions, necessary for a *Salam* contract, is that full payment must be made by the buyer at the time of effecting the sale.   **T   F**
38. With a *Salam* contract the *Rab ul Mall* has a completely certain rate of return.   **T   F**
39. With a *Salam* contract the *Rab ul Mall* has a completely uncertain rate of return.   **T   F**
40. With a *Salam* contract the *Rab ul Mall* has an uncertain rate of return for a short period only.   **T   F**
41. With a *Salam* contract the cost of capital, for the *Rab ul Mall*, is completely fixed and predetermined.   **T   F**
42. With a *Salam* contract the cost of capital, for the *Rab ul Mall*, is completely uncertain until the end of the contract.   **T   F**
43. With a *Salam* contract the *Rab ul Mall* has a completely certain rate of return.   **T   F**
44. With a *Salam* contract the *Rab ul Mall* has a completely uncertain rate of return.   **T   F**
45. With a *Salam* contract the *Rab ul Mall* has an uncertain rate of return for a short period only.   **T   F**
46. With a *Salam* contract the cost of capital, for the *Rab ul Mall*, is completely fixed and predetermined.   **T   F**
47. With a *Salam* contract the cost of capital, for the *Rab ul Mall*, is completely uncertain until the end of the contract.   **T   F**
48. One of the *Sharia'a* conditions necessary for a *Salam* contract is that, in the event of a harvest failure, the *Salam* contract is nullified.   **T   F**
49. One of the *Sharia'a* conditions necessary for a *Salam* contract is that, in the event of a harvest failure, the *Salam* contract must still be fulfilled.   **T   F**
50. *Salam* is a *Sharia'a*-compliant Islamic mode of finance because the risk is such that the financial institution and the client have to share the losses in proportion to the respective capital contributions.   **T   F**
51. Under a *Salam* contract the *Rab ul Mall* has no control over the management of the funds.   **T   F**
52. Under a *Salam* contract the *Rab ul Mall* has full control over the management of the funds.   **T   F**
53. *Salam* is a *Sharia'a*-compliant mode of finance given that the risk is such that if the *Rab ul Mall*'s client does not pay on time, or does not pay at all, the *Rab ul Mall* is at risk.   **T   F**
54. *Salam* is a *Sharia'a*-compliant mode of finance given that the risk is such that if the leased asset is destroyed, without any misuse or negligence on the part of the lessee, it is the *Rab ul Mall* (lessor) who must bear the risk.   **T   F**
55. *Salam* is a *Sharia'a*-compliant mode of finance given that the risk is such that if the manufacturer, who has agreed to manufacture the goods, makes faulty goods, or does not deliver them on time, the *Rab ul Mall* is at risk.   **T   F**

9.2.3   *Istisna'a* and *Salam* Contracts

56. *Istisna'a* is an Arabic term which means a 'deferred credit sale'.   **T   F**
57. *Istisna'a* is an Arabic term which means 'an order to manufacture a specific physical asset for the purchaser'.   **T   F**
58. *Istisna'a* is an Arabic term which means 'an agreement to provide working capital for business'.   **T   F**
59. Under an *Istisna'a* contract, *al-musania'a* means the asset that must be built.   **T   F**
60. Under an *Istisna'a* contract, *al-mustasni* means the manufacturer of the asset.   **T   F**
61. Under an *Istisna'a* contract, *al-mustasni* means the buyer of the asset.   **T   F**

62. *Istisna'a* can only be used for agricultural projects.   **T   F**
63. *Istisna'a* can only be used for manufacturing projects.   **T   F**
64. *Istisna'a* consists of a contract whereby a *Rab ul Mall* enters into a contract with the entrepreneur/buyer.   **T   F**
65. *Istisna'a* consists of a contract whereby a *Rab ul Mall* enters into a contract with the manufacturer/contractor.   **T   F**
66. Under an *Istisna'a* contract, a bank's role is that of *Rab ul Mall*/seller.   **T   F**
67. Under an *Istisna'a* contract, a *Rab ul Mall*'s role is that of borrower/lender.   **T   F**
68. One difference between *Istisna'a* and *Murabaha* is that, with a *Murabaha* contract, a customer can only buy the goods when they are constructed.   **T   F**
69. One difference between *Istisna'a* and *Murabaha* is that, with a *Murabaha* contract, a customer can buy the goods before they are constructed.   **T   F**
70. One difference between *Istisna'a* and *Murabaha* is that, with an *Istisna'a* contract, the *Rab ul Mall* can buy the goods before they are constructed.   **T   F**
71. One difference between *Istisna'a* and *Salam* is that an *Istisna'a* contract refers to something needing manufacturing whereas a *Salam* contract does not.   **T   F**
72. One difference between *Istisna'a* and *Salam* is that under a *Salam* contract the full price is paid to the deliverer of the goods in advance.   **T   F**
73. Under a *Salam* contract, agricultural goods are sold before they are grown, therefore they are not *Sharia'a* compliant.   **T   F**
74. Under a *Salam* contract, a seller must deliver the goods as agreed on the due date.   **T   F**
75. Under a *Salam* contract, a seller assumes full responsibilities for delivery at the agreed price.   **T   F**
76. One of the benefits to a seller, with a *Salam* contract, is that he is not responsible in the event that bad weather destroys his crops.   **T   F**
77. One of the benefits to a seller, with a *Salam* contract, is that he gets paid in advance.   **T   F**
78. One of the benefits to a seller, with a *Salam* contract, is that he can cancel the contract and sell the goods to another buyer if prices have risen meanwhile.   **T   F**
79. Under the *Sharia'a*, one cannot normally sell something that does not currently exist.   **T   F**
80. Under a *Salam* contract, goods are sold before they are grown, and therefore they are not *Sharia'a* compliant.   **T   F**
81. Under an *Istisna'a* contract, goods are sold before they are manufactured, and therefore they are not *Sharia'a* compliant.   **T   F**

9.2.4   Risks with the *Salam* Contract

Describe at least two risks associated with the *Salam* contract:

Risk 1

_____

_____

_____

_____

_____

_____

Risk 2

_____

_____

_____

_____

_____

_____

9.3   ANSWERS

9.3.1   What are the Features of the *Salam* Contract

1. How does *Salam* work?

    The bank buys real goods that it can then sell in the market. The bank pays spot and receives the goods in the future.

2. In what sense is *Salam* an asset-based or equity-based source of finance?

    Money has no intrinsic utility in Islam; it is only a medium of exchange. Making money from money is *riba* and thereby *haram*. Financing in Islam must be asset based or equity based. The asset created must be intrinsically illiquid. As it says in the *Qur'an*: 'Allah has permitted trade and prohibited *riba*'.

    The bank has bought real goods (e.g. wheat), making it asset based.

3. What is the risk for the *Rab ul Mall* providing the finance?

    Islam requires that any *Rab ul Mall* profits are only justified if there is risk preference by investors. This is based on the Arabic term *Al Ghunm bil-Ghurm*, i.e., profits must be linked with the investors' willingness to take risk.

    There is the risk that goods are never delivered at the agreed future date. There is also the risk that the *Rab ul Mall* cannot sell the goods for a profit either now or in the future.

9.3.2   The *Salam* Contract

4. A. FALSE
   B. TRUE
   C. FALSE
5. A. TRUE
   B. TRUE
   C. TRUE
6. A. FALSE
   B. FALSE
   C. TRUE
7. A. FALSE
   B. TRUE
   C. FALSE
8. A. TRUE
   B. TRUE
   C. FALSE

9. A. TRUE
    B. TRUE
    C. FALSE
    D. FALSE
10. A. FALSE
    B. TRUE
    C. FALSE
11. A. FALSE
    B. FALSE
    C. TRUE
12. A. TRUE
    B. FALSE
    C. FALSE
13. TRUE
14. FALSE
15. FALSE
16. TRUE
17. TRUE
18. FALSE
19. FALSE
20. FALSE
21. TRUE
22. FALSE
23. FALSE
24. TRUE
25. TRUE
26. FALSE
27. TRUE
28. TRUE
29. FALSE
30. FALSE
31. TRUE
32. TRUE
33. TRUE
34. FALSE
35. FALSE
36. TRUE
37. TRUE
38. FALSE
39. TRUE
40. FALSE
41. TRUE
42. FALSE
43. FALSE
44. TRUE
45. FALSE
46. TRUE

47. FALSE
48. FALSE
49. TRUE
50. FALSE
51. TRUE
52. FALSE
53. FALSE
54. FALSE
55. FALSE

9.3.3   *Istisna'a* and *Salam* Contracts

56. FALSE
57. TRUE
58. FALSE
59. FALSE
60. FALSE
61. TRUE
62. FALSE
63. TRUE
64. TRUE
65. TRUE
66. TRUE
67. FALSE
68. TRUE
69. FALSE
70. TRUE
71. TRUE
72. TRUE
73. FALSE
74. TRUE
75. TRUE
76. FALSE
77. TRUE
78. FALSE
79. TRUE
80. FALSE
81. FALSE

9.3.4   Risks with the *Salam* Contract

Risk 1 *Credit Risk*: Settlement/delivery risk where the goods are not delivered or not delivered on time.

Risk 2 *Market Risk*: The risk that if there is a default then the bank has to purchase the goods on the open market at a higher price than the agreed price in the Parallel *Salam* contract.

10

Takaful: Islamic Insurance

10.1 LEARNING OUTCOMES, SUMMARY OVERVIEW AND PROBLEMS

10.1.1 Learning Outcomes

After reading Chapter 10 you should be able to do the following:

- Define the concept of *Takaful*.
- Define the concept of Re*Takaful*.
- Explain the Islamic issues with conventional insurance.
- Contrast *Takaful* with Re*Takaful*.
- Describe *Tabarru'*.
- Explain the *Sharia'a* issues with *Takaful*.
- Identify the parties to a *Takaful* contract.
- Explain the Islamic origins of *Takaful*.
- Describe the *Ta'awun* model of *Takaful*.
- Describe the nonprofit model of *Takaful*.
- Describe the *Mudaraba* model of *Takaful*.
- Describe the *Wakala* model of *Takaful*.
- Describe the hybrid model of *Takaful*.
- Explain the role of *Sharia'a* boards within the *Takaful* industry.
- Contrast conventional reinsurance with Re*Takaful*.
- Test that you have fully understood the principles that underlie the applications of *Takaful* within the insurance industry.

10.1.2 Summary Overview

Takaful is an Islamic insurance concept grounded in Islamic *Muamalat* (banking transactions), observing the rules and regulations of Islamic law. This concept has been practised in various forms for over 1400 years. Muslim Jurists acknowledge that the basis of shared responsibility in the system of *Aquila* (blood money), as practised between the Muslims of Mecca and Medina, laid the foundation of mutual insurance.

10.1.2.1 Principles of Takaful

The principles of *Takaful* are as follows:

- Policyholders cooperate among themselves for their common good.
- Every policyholder pays his subscription to help those that need assistance.
- Losses are divided and liabilities spread according to a community pooling system.
- Uncertainty is eliminated in respect of subscription and compensation.
- No members derive an advantage at the cost of others.

Theoretically, *Takaful* is perceived as cooperative or mutual insurance, where members contribute a certain sum of money to a common pool. The purpose of this system is not profits but to uphold the principle of 'bear ye one another's burden'.

Convention insurance, as agreed upon by most contemporary scholars, is not allowed for Muslims because it contains the following *haram* elements:

- *gharar* (uncertainty);
- *maisir* (gambling);
- *riba* (interest).

There are three models and several variations on how *Takaful* can be implemented:

- *Mudaraba* model;
- *Wakala* model;
- combination of both – a hybrid model.

10.1.2.2   Islamic Insurance (Takaful) Companies

The demand for Islamic insurance over recent years, particularly within the Gulf Cooperation Council (GCC) countries and other areas of the Middle East, has seen a proliferation of new companies offering Islamic insurance products in these markets. The majority of these companies are fully fledged *Takaful* operators, but conventional insurance companies have also entered the market with *Takaful* 'window' operations.

10.1.3   *Takaful* Products are Based on Three Main Business Models

10.1.3.1   The Mudaraba Model

This is essentially a basis for sharing profit and loss between the *Takaful* operator and the policyholders. The *Takaful* operator manages the operation in return for a share of the surplus on underwriting and a share of profit from the returns on investments. This model is commonly used in Malaysia.

By this principle, the entrepreneur or *Mudarib* (*Takaful* operator) will accept payment of the *Takaful* instalments or *Takaful* contributions (premium) termed *Ras ul Mall* from investors or providers of capital or fund (*Takaful* participants) acting as *Sahib-ul-Mal*.

The contract specifies how the profit (surplus) from the operations of *Takaful* managed by the *Takaful* operator is to be shared, in accordance with the principle of *Mudaraba*, between the participants as the providers of capital and the *Takaful* operator as the entrepreneur. The sharing of such profit may be in a ratio of 50:50, 60:40, 70:30 or whatever is mutually agreed between the contracting parties.

In order to eliminate the element of uncertainty in the *Takaful* contract, the concept of *tabarru'* (to donate, to contribute, to give away) is incorporated.

In relation to this concept, a participant agrees to relinquish as *tabarru'*, a certain proportion of his *Takaful* instalments or contributions that he agrees or undertakes to pay should any of his fellow participants suffer a defined loss. This agreement enables him to fulfil his obligation of mutual help and joint guarantee.

In essence, *tabarru'* enables the participants to perform their deeds in sincerely assisting fellow participants who might suffer a loss or damage due to a catastrophe or disaster.

The sharing of profit or surplus that may emerge from the operations of *Takaful* is made only after the obligation of assisting the fellow participants has been fulfilled. It is imperative, therefore, for a *Takaful* operator to maintain adequate assets of the defined funds under their care while simultaneously striving prudently to ensure that the funds are sufficiently protected against undue over-exposure.

Mudaraba is the commercial profit-sharing contract between the provider or providers of funds for a business venture and the entrepreneur who actually conducts the business. The operation of *Takaful* may thus be envisaged as a profit-sharing business venture between the *Takaful* operator and the individual members of a group of participants who desire to guarantee each other reciprocally against a certain loss or damage that may be inflicted upon any one of them.

Under the *Mudaraba* principle, the profit as universally defined by conventional insurance companies, which in the case of general business is taken to mean returns on investment plus underwriting surplus, is then shared according to a mutually agreed ratio between the participants and the operators. Management expenses of the operator including agency remuneration, if any, shall be borne by the shareholders' fund and not from the *Takaful* funds. Hence, there is a distinct separation between *Takaful* funds and shareholders' funds.

10.1.3.2   The **Wakala** *Model*

This is a contract of agency, which replaces surplus sharing with a performance fee. The *Takaful* operator in this case acts as an agent (*Wakeel*) for participants and manages the *Takaful*/Re*Takaful* fund in return for a defined fee. This model is used more in the Middle East region.

Under the *Wakala* principle, the paid-up capital is contributed as a donation by the shareholders. Therefore, under this principle the shareholders do not expect and probably do not mind not receiving any returns on the capital donated. However, certain scholars have recently argued that the shareholders (operators) in their capacity as managers should also be entitled to share the profit arising from the *Takaful* business.

On a strict interpretation of the *Wakala* model, the surplus of policyholders' funds investments (net of the management fee or expenses) goes to the policyholders.

The shareholders charge a *Wakala* fee from contributions that covers most of the expenses of business. The fee rate is fixed annually in advance in consultation with the *Sharia'a* board of the company. In order to give an incentive for good governance the management fee is usually related to the level of performance.

10.1.3.3   *Hybrid* **Wakala/Mudaraba** *Model*

According to this hybrid model, *Takaful* insurance contracts are issued under the *Wakala* model, while *Mudaraba* is applied for investment activities.

10.2   QUESTIONS

10.2.1   *Takaful* **Terminology and Concepts**

1. Is the concept of insurance *haram* in Islam?
2. Why is conventional insurance considered *haram* for Muslims?

3. Why do Muslims need *Takaful* if everything that happens in this world is by the will of Allah (*Qada'* and *Qadar*)?
4. Is *Takaful Sharia'a* compliant?
5. What is *Takaful*?
6. How does *Takaful* work?
7. What is the *Ta'awun* model?
8. What are the differences between *Takaful* and non-*Takaful* forms of insurance?
9. What happens if there is a surplus in the *Takaful* fund?
10. How does the *Mudaraba* model of *Takaful* work?
11. How does the *Wakala* model of *Takaful* work?
12. How does the *Takaful waqf* model work?
13. What are the two separate funds in *Takaful*?
14. What is Family *Takaful*?
15. How does Family *Takaful* work?
16. What happens when the policyholder dies with Family *Takaful*?
17. What is General *Takaful*?

10.2.2   *Takaful* Principles

Circle true (T) or false (F) in the statements below. Note that you need to indicate T or F for each statement.

18. In determining any compensation, the *Takaful* operator will identify the cause of the loss. **T   F**
19. A *Takaful* contract is based on the principle of utmost good faith (trust), whereby participants do not need to disclose all material information required.   **T   F**
20. After participants have been compensated for any loss, the *Takaful* operator has no right to claim from any third party responsible for the loss.   **T   F**
21. Participants must have a legitimate financial interest in the subject matter in order to participate in a *Takaful* plan.   **T   F**
22. A *Takaful* contract is based on the principle of utmost good faith (trust), whereby participants need to disclose all material information required.   **T   F**
23. After participants have been compensated for any loss, the *Takaful* operator has the right to claim from any third party responsible for the loss.   **T   F**
24. Participants can only recover any financial loss and not gain any profit as a result of a quantifiable loss in a *Takaful* plan.   **T   F**
25. In determining any compensation, the *Takaful* operator is not concerned with the cause of the loss in a *Takaful* plan.   **T   F**
26. Participants do not need a legitimate financial interest in the subject matter to participate in a *Takaful* plan.   **T   F**
27. Participants can recover any financial loss and may also make a profit as a result of a quantifiable loss in a *Takaful* plan.   **T   F**
28. The majority of *Sharia'a* scholars consider conventional insurance to be prohibited (*haram*) and inconsistent with *Sharia'a* principles for six main reasons:
   A. It includes the element of uncertainty (*gharar*).   **T   F**
   B. All is prohibited unless it is specifically permitted.   **T   F**
   C. It includes the element of gambling (*maisir*).   **T   F**

D. It includes the elements of interest-bearing investments and usury (*riba*).   **T   F**

E. It may include investments in non-*Sharia'a*-compliant projects or financial instruments.   **T   F**

F. 'Buyer beware' is an important principle in Islam.   **T   F**

29. *Sharia'a* requires the following:

A. Risk and reward sharing.   **T   F**

B. *Fatawa* to be consistent.   **T   F**

C. Fairness and transparency.   **T   F**

D. Sanctity of contracts.   **T   F**

E. All is permissible unless it is specifically prohibited.   **T   F**

F. Training of new scholars.   **T   F**

10.3   ANSWERS

10.3.1   *Takaful* Terminology and Concepts

1. Is the concept of insurance, *haram* in Islam?

   The concept of insurance is not *haram* in Islam when undertaken in the framework of *Takaful* or mutual cooperation and solidarity. Contrary to conventional insurance, *Takaful* does not contain *Sharia'a* nonpermissible elements such as *gharar* (uncertainty), gambling and investing in interest-bearing instruments.

2. Why is conventional insurance considered *haram* for Muslims?

   Conventional insurance is based on a contract of exchange (sale) between the insurance company and the insured person. This contract is void because it has one or all of the following elements, which are not permissible from a *Sharia'a* perspective:

   Gharar (uncertainty): Conventional insurance has an element of *gharar* due to the promise to pay a sum of money upon the occurrence of unexpected events.

   Maisir (gambling): The existence of *gharar* (uncertainty) leads to *maisir* in conventional insurance. The insured may either lose all the premiums he has paid or be compensated for the losses he incurs for the insured event.

   Riba (usury/interest): The investments of conventional insurance funds in interest-bearing securities such as bonds, which do not comply with *Sharia'a* principles, pose a major problem for Muslims who purchase conventional insurance.

3. Why do Muslims need *Takaful* if everything that happens in this world is by the will of Allah (*Qada'* and *Qadar*)?

   The taking out of a *Takaful* policy is not superseding the power or will of Allah in one's life, death or destiny (*Qada'* and *Qadar*), but is achieving the pleasure of Allah who orders Muslims to 'help . . . one another in righteousness and piety'. The main objective of *Takaful* is to provide a level of comfort to the participants against unexpected future risk, with this being achieved through mutual cooperation.

4. Is *Takaful Sharia'a* compliant?

   Takaful is *Sharia'a* compliant because it is based on the principle of cooperation, not sale or exchange, and mitigates the objectionable aspects of *gharar, maisir* and *riba*. This is contrary to conventional insurance, where policyholders pay premiums as a price for protection against a catastrophe. If a catastrophe occurs, the policyholder will be protected. The policyholder will still sacrifice the premium to the insurance company if such a catastrophe does not occur.

In contrast, a contribution to a *Takaful* fund is an agreement with other members (participants) of the fund to help each other mutually by way of providing financial assistance should any member of the fund suffer a catastrophe or disaster. Moreover a *Takaful* fund invests the contributions in a *Sharia'a*-compliant manner avoiding any interest-based instruments. In addition, any surplus will be redistributed to the participants.

The *Takaful* operator therefore only manages this pool (for a fee) for the benefit of the members/participants.

5. What is *Takaful*?

Takaful means 'guaranteeing each other' and is based on the principles of *Ta'awun* (mutual cooperation) and *Tabarru'* (donation). In this arrangement, a group of *Takaful* participants (policyholders) agree between themselves to share the risk of a potential loss to any of them, by making a donation of all or part of their *Takaful* contribution (premium) to compensate for a loss.

In conventional insurance the risk is transferred from the policyholder to the insurance company, which brings elements of uncertainty and chance into the contract as to if and when one of the two parties makes a loss. *Takaful* is a structure in which the risk is shared between all participants, thus removing the elements of uncertainty and gambling from the contract.

6. How does *Takaful* work?

The participants of *Takaful* each pay a *Takaful* contribution, based on their individual risk and the likelihood of making a claim, to create a *Takaful* fund. The nature of the risk covered, and the period of cover, is specified in the *Takaful* contract (insurance policy).

The *Takaful* fund is invested strictly in *halal* activities, with non-interest bearing assets, in order to maximise the fund value in a *Sharia'a*-compliant manner.

If it is ascertained that the *Takaful* fund is overfunded, the amount by which it is overfunded will be distributed to eligible *Takaful* participants by way of a participation discount (in addition to any No Claims Discount) from the participants' next year's *Takaful* contribution.

7. What is the *Ta'awun* model?

The *Ta'awun* model (cooperative insurance) practises the concept of *Mudaraba* in daily transactions, where it encourages the Islamic values of brotherhood, unity, solidarity and mutual cooperation. In the *Mudaraba* model, the *Takaful* operator and the participant share the direct investment income, while the participant is entitled to 100% of the surplus, with no deduction made prior to any distributions.

8. What are the differences between *Takaful* and non-*Takaful* forms of insurance?

The major differences are summarised in Table 10.1.

9. What happens if there is a surplus in the *Takaful* fund?

One unique aspect of *Takaful* is the sharing of any surplus of the *Takaful* fund among the participants. A portion of the surplus must be returned to the participants. The surplus is calculated after deducting expenses such as claims, net re-*Takaful* costs and changes in the technical reserves.

10. How does the *Takaful Mudaraba* model work?

This is a profit and loss sharing model. The participant and the *Takaful* insurer share the surplus. The sharing of such profit (surplus) differs based on a ratio, mutually agreed to in advance, between the contracting parties. Generally, these risk sharing arrangements allow the *Takaful* insurer to share in the underwriting results from operations, as well as any favourable performance returns on invested premiums.

Table 10.1   Differences between *Takaful* and non-*Takaful* forms of insurance

	Takaful	Conventional insurance
The contract	The contract among participants of the *Takaful* fund is the contract of *tabarru'* (donation, gift) and therefore is about cooperation and mutual help among them. *Takaful* contracts are very transparent.	This is a contract of exchange, i.e., a Sale and Purchase agreement between the insurer (the company) and the insured-upon, which the insured buys and the insurer sells.
Responsibility for providing protection	Participants are responsible for protecting each other through *tabarru'*. The *Takaful* operator only manages the *Takaful* operations on behalf of participants.	Non-*Takaful* companies, other than mutual companies, provide protection in return for premiums. Policyholders have no relationship among themselves though they contribute to the same insurance fund.
Surplus	The *Takaful* surplus belongs to the participants. A portion of the surplus is to be distributed back to the participants.	Any surplus belongs to the insurer.
Liability of the insurer/operator	The *Takaful* operator, acting on behalf of the participants, pays claims from the *Takaful* fund.	The insurer is responsible for paying claims from its assets (insurance funds and shareholders' fund).
Investment	All funds are invested in *Sharia'a*-compliant investments.	Funds received may be invested in both *Sharia'a* and non-*Sharia'a* compliant investments.

11. How does the *Takaful Wakala* model work?

    This is a fee-based model. Cooperative risk sharing occurs among participants where a *Takaful* insurer simply earns a fee for services (as a *Wakeel*, or 'agent') and does not participate or share in any underwriting outcomes. The insurer's fee may include a fund management fee and a performance incentive fee.

12. How does the *Takaful waqf* model work?

    Unlike the *Mudaraba* and *Wakala* models, *waqf* operates as a social/ governmental enterprise, and programmes are operated on a nonprofit basis. Under the *waqf* model, any surplus or profit is not owned directly by either the insurer or the participants, and there is no mechanism to distribute any surplus funds. In effect, the insurer retains the surplus funds to support the participants community.

13. What are the two separate funds in *Takaful*?

    First, there is a *Takaful* (or policyholders') fund and second an operator's (or shareholders') fund. The *Takaful* fund operates under pure cooperative principles, in a very similar way to conventional mutual insurance entities. Underwriting deficits and surpluses are accrued over time within this fund, to which the operator has no direct recourse.

    As a result, the *Takaful* fund effectively is ring-fenced and protected from the potential default of the operator's fund. Management expenses and seed capital are borne by the operator's fund, where the main income takes the form of either a predefined management fee (to cover costs) or a share of investment returns and underwriting results (or a combination of both).

14. What is Family *Takaful*?

Family *Takaful* provides members with protection and long-term savings. Members, or their beneficiaries, will be provided with financial benefits if they suffer a tragedy. At the same time, they enjoy a long-term personal savings plan because part of their contribution is deposited in an account for the purpose of saving. Members will be able to enjoy investment returns from the savings portion based on a pre-agreed ratio.

15. How does Family *Takaful* work?

When members participate in Family *Takaful*, they contribute a certain amount of money to a *Takaful* fund. They undertake a contract (*aqd*) for part of their contribution to be in the form of participative contribution (*tabarru'*) and the other part for savings and investment.

The contribution, in the form of *tabarru'*, is placed in a fund, the Participants' Special Account (PSA), which is used to fulfil any obligation of mutual help, should any of the participants face misfortune arising from death or permanent disability. If members survive until the date of maturity of the plan, they are entitled to share the net surplus from the fund, if there is any.

The *Takaful* operator invests the savings and investment contribution, the Participant's Account (PA), and the profit is shared between the member and the *Takaful* operator according to a pre-agreed ratio.

16. What happens when the policy holder dies with Family *Takaful*?

If members pass away before their *Takaful* plan matures, the *Takaful* operator will pay to their nominee (*wasi*) the following benefits:

1. From the Participant Account (PA): The amount accumulated in the PA plus the share of profits from the date of inception of the *Takaful* plan to the due date of payment prior to death.
2. From the Participant Savings Account (PSA): The sum covered under the risk or *tabarru'* portion.

If members survive until the date of maturity, they will be entitled to the following benefits:

From the PA: the amount accumulated in the PA plus the share of profits from the investment.

From the PSA: the net surplus allocated, if there is any.

17. What is general *Takaful*?

This is to cover everyday risks including the following:

Motor insurance:

Cars, motorcycles, taxis, commercial vehicles, industrial and agricultural vehicles.

Building insurance:

Residential properties including houses, flats and holiday homes.

Commercial properties including offices, shops and factories.

Community buildings including mosques and schools.

Contents insurance:

Household contents, personal effects and valuables.

Business insurance:

Business premises – fire and theft etc.; stock, equipment and materials; employer's liability; public liability; loss of revenue; professional indemnity.

10.3.2   *Takaful* **Principles**

18. **TRUE**
19. **FALSE**
20. **FALSE**
21. **TRUE**
22. **TRUE**
23. **TRUE**
24. **TRUE**
25. **FALSE**
26. **FALSE**
27. **FALSE**
28. A. **TRUE**
    B. **FALSE**
    C. **TRUE**
    D. **TRUE**
    E. **TRUE**
    F. **FALSE**
29. A. **TRUE**
    B. **FALSE**
    C. **TRUE**
    D. **TRUE**
    E. **TRUE**
    F. **FALSE**

Glossary

This glossary provides the key terms used in Islamic banking and finance. (A bold/italic term in a definition indicates that the word is defined elsewhere in the Glossary.)

Amanah: This refers to deposits held in trust. A person can hold a property in trust for another, sometimes by express contract and sometimes by implication of a contract. *Amanah* entails an absence of liability for loss except in the breach of duty. Current accounts are regarded as *Amanah* (trust). If the bank gets authority to use current accounts funds in its business, *Amanah* transforms into a loan. As every loan has to be repaid, banks are liable to repay the full amount of the current accounts.

Arbun: Down payment. A non-refundable deposit paid by a buyer retaining a right to confirm or cancel the sale.

Bai' Muajjal: Literally this means a credit sale. Technically, it is a financing technique adopted by Islamic banks that takes the form of **Murabaha** *Muajjal*. It is a contract in which the seller earns a profit margin on his purchase price and allows the buyer to pay the price of the commodity at a future date in a lump sum or in instalments. He has to mention expressly the cost of the commodity and the margin of profit is mutually agreed upon.

Bai' al-'Inah: A contract that involves the sale and buy-back transaction of assets by a seller. A seller sells the asset to a buyer on a cash basis. The seller later buys back the same asset on a deferred payment basis where the price is higher than the cash price.

Bai' al-Istijrar: A contract between the client and the supplier, whereby the supplier agrees to supply a particular produce on an ongoing basis, for example monthly, at an agreed price and on the basis of an agreed mode of payment.

Bai' al-Dayn: A transaction that involves the sale and purchase of securities or debt certificates that complies with the **Sharia'a**. Securities or debt certificates will be issued by a debtor to a creditor as evidence of indebtedness.

Bai' al-Muzayadah: An action by a person to sell an asset in the open market, which is accompanied by the process of bidding among potential buyers. The asset for sale will be awarded to the person who has offered the highest price.

Bai' bil Wafa: Sale with a right of the seller enabling him to repurchase (redeem) the property by refunding the purchase price. According to the majority of *Fuqaha* this is not permissible.

Bai' Bithaman Ajil (BBA): A contract that refers to the sale and purchase transactions for the financing of assets on a deferred and an instalment basis with a pre-agreed payment period. The sale price will include a profit margin.

Dayn (debt): A *Dayn* comes into existence as a result of a contract or credit transaction. It is incurred by way of rent, sale, purchase or in any other way that leaves it as a debt to another. *Duyun* (debts) should be repaid without any profit to the lender because they are advanced to help the needy and meet their demands and, therefore, the lender should not impose on the borrower more than he was given on credit.

Dhaman: Contract of guarantee, security or collateral.

Family Takaful: This arrangement provides members, or their beneficiaries, with financial protection: they will be provided with monetary benefits if they suffer a tragedy. Members can also enjoy long-term investment returns from the savings portion based on a pre-agreed ratio.

Fiqh: Islamic law. The science of the *Sharia'a*. Practical jurisprudence or human articulations of divine rules encompassing both law and ethics. *Fiqh* may be understood as the Jurists' understanding of the *Sharia'a*, or Jurists' law. *Fiqh al-Muamalat* is Islamic commercial jurisprudence, or the rules for transacting in a *Sharia'a*-compliant manner. This is an important source of Islamic banking and economics.

Gharar: Any element of absolute or excessive uncertainty in any business or contract. *Gharar* potentially leads to undue loss to a party and unjustified enrichment of another. This is prohibited under the *Sharia'a*.

Al Ghunm bil Ghurm: This provides the rationale and the principle of profit sharing in *Shirkah* arrangements. Earning profit is legitimised only by engaging in an economic venture involving risk sharing that ultimately contributes to economic development.

Halal: Anything permitted by the *Sharia'a*.

Haram: Anything prohibited by the *Sharia'a*.

Hawalah: Literally, this means transfer. Legally, it is an agreement by which a debtor is freed from a debt by another party becoming responsible for it or by the transfer of a claim of a debt shifting the responsibility from one person to another. It also refers to the document by which the transfer takes place.

Hibah: Gift.

Ijara: Leasing. This is the sale of a definite usufruct of any asset in exchange for definite reward. It refers to a contract under which Islamic banks lease equipment, buildings or other facilities to a client, against an agreed rental.

Ijara wa Iqtina: A mode of financing, by way of hire purchase, adopted by Islamic banks. It is a contract under which an Islamic bank finances equipment, buildings or other facilities for the client against an agreed rental together with a unilateral undertaking by the bank or the client that, at the end of the lease period, the ownership in the asset will be transferred to the lessee. The undertaking, or the promise, does not become an integral part of the lease contract in order to make it conditional. The rental, as well as the purchase price, is fixed in such a manner that the bank gets back its principal sum along with some profit. This is usually determined in advance.

Ijtihad: An endeavour of a qualified Jurist to derive or formulate a rule of law to determine the true ruling of the divine law in a matter on which the revelation is not explicit or certain. This would be on the basis of *Nass* (evidence) found in the *Qur'an* and the *Sunnah*.

Ijma: Consensus of all or a majority of the leading qualified Jurists on a certain *Sharia'a* matter at a certain moment in time.

'Inah: A double sale by which the borrower and the lender sell and then resell an object between them, once for cash and once for a higher price on credit, with the net result being a loan with interest.

'Inan *(type of* **Sharikah***)*: A form of partnership in which each partner contributes capital and has a right to work for the business, not necessarily equally.

Istihsan: A doctrine of Islamic law that allows exceptions to strict legal reasoning, or guiding choice among possible legal outcomes, when considerations of human welfare so demand.

Istisna'a: A contractual agreement for manufacturing goods and commodities, allowing cash payment in advance and future delivery or a future payment and future delivery. A manufacturer or builder agrees to produce or build a well described good or building at a given price on a given date in the future. The price can be paid in instalments, step by step as agreed between the parties. *Istisna'a* can be used for financing the manufacture or construction of houses, plant, projects and the building of bridges, roads and power stations.

Iwad: An equivalent counter-value or recompense. This is an important principle of Islamic finance. Contracts without *iwad* are not Islamically acceptable.

Jahala: Ignorance, lack of knowledge; indefiniteness in a contract, sometimes leading to *gharar*.

Jua'alah: Literally, *Jua'alah* constitutes wages, pay, stipend or reward. Legally, it is a contract for performing a given task against a prescribed fee in a given period. *Ujrah* is a similar contract in which any work is done against a stipulated wage or fee.

Kafalah **(suretyship):** Literally, *Kafalah* means responsibility, or suretyship. Legally in *Kafalah* a third party becomes a surety for the payment of debt. It is a pledge given to a creditor that the debtor will pay the debt or fine. Suretyship in Islamic law is the creation of an additional liability with regard to the claim, not to the debt itself.

Khiyar: Option or a power to annul or cancel a contract.

Maisir: An ancient Arabian game of chance played with arrows without heads and feathers, for stakes of slaughtered and quartered camels. It came to be identified with all types of gambling.

al-masnoo: The subject matter of an *Istisna'a* contract.

al-musania'a: The seller/manufacturer in an *Istisna'a* contract.

al-muslam: The buyer in a *Salam* contract.

al-muslam fihi: The commodity to be delivered in a *Salam* contract.

al-muslam ileihi: The seller in a *Salam* contract.

al-mustasni: The ultimate buyer in an *Istisna'a* contract.

Mithli **(fungible goods):** Goods that can be returned in kind, that is gold for gold, silver for silver, US$ for US$, wheat for wheat and so on.

Mujtahid: Legal expert, or a Jurist who expends great effort in deriving a legal opinion interpreting the sources of *Sharia'a* law.

Mudaraba **(trust financing):** An agreement made between two parties one of whom provides 100% of the capital for the project and who has no control over the management of the project, and another party know as a *Mudarib*, who manages the project using his entrepreneurial skills. Profits arising from the project are distributed according to a predetermined ratio. Losses are borne by the provider of capital.

Mudarib: The managing partner in a *Mudaraba* contract.

Mujir: The lessor – a person or institution who provides an asset with an *Ijara* (lease).

Murabaha (cost plus financing): A contract sale between the bank and its client for the sale of goods at a price that includes a profit margin agreed by both parties. As a financing technique it involves the purchase of goods by the bank as requested by its client. The goods are sold to the client with an agreed mark-up.

Musawamah: A general kind of sale in which the price of the commodity to be traded is arrived at by bargaining between the seller and the purchaser without any reference to the price paid or cost incurred by the former.

Musharaka (joint venture financing): This Islamic financing technique involves a joint venture between two parties who both provide capital for the financing of a project. Both parties share profits on a pre-agreed ratio, but losses are shared on the basis of equity participation. Management of the project may be carried out by both the parties or by just one party. This is a very flexible arrangement where the sharing of the profits and management can be negotiated and pre-agreed by all parties.

Musharik: Professional who manages the transactions under the *Musharaka* mode of financing

Mustajir: The lessee – a person (or institution) to whom an asset with an *Ijara* (lease) is provided.

Mutajara: Deposits made by banks in Saudi Arabia to SAMA, the central bank.

Muwakkil: The person who appoints the *Wakil* in a *Wakala* contract.

Qard (**loan of fungible objects**)*:* Legally, *Qard* means to give something of value without expecting any return. *Qard* can provide help, charity or money needed for a specific occasion (death, wedding and so on). No monetary return is expected although the finance must be repaid. The Prophet is reported to have said '. . .every loan must be paid. . .'. But if a debtor is in difficulty, the creditor is expected to extend time or even voluntarily remit the whole or a part of the principal. The literal meaning of *Qard* is to cut. It is so called because the property is really cut off when it is given to the borrower.

Qimar: Gambling. Technically, it is an arrangement in which possession of something of value is contingent upon the happening of an uncertain event. By implication it applies to a situation in which there is a loss for one party and a gain for the other without specifying which party will lose and which will gain.

Qiyas: Literally, this means measure, example, comparison or analogy. Technically, it means a derivation of the law on the analogy of an existing law if the basis (*'ilaih*) of the two is the same. It is one of the sources of *Sharia'a* law.

Rab ul Mall: Capital investor/finance provider.

Rahn: (pledge or collateral). Legally, *Rahn* means to pledge or lodge a real or corporeal property of material value, in accordance with the law, as security, for a debt or pecuniary obligation so as to make it possible for the creditor to recover the debt or some portion of the goods or property. In the pre-Islamic contracts, *Rahn* implied a type of 'earnest money', which was lodged as a guarantee and material evidence or proof of a contract, especially when there was no scribe available to confirm this in writing.

Ras ul Mall: Capital (cost) paid (in cash, kind or benefit) in both *Salam* and *Istisna'a* contracts; i.e., the price paid.

Riba: An excess or increase. Technically, it means an increase over principal in a loan transaction or in exchange for a commodity accrued to the owner (lender) without giving an equivalent counter-value or recompense (*'iwad*), in return, to the other party. *Riba* means an increase that is without an *'iwad* or equal counter-value.

Riba Al-Fadl: '*Riba* in excess': the quality premium when exchanging low quality with better quality goods, for example, dates for dates, wheat for wheat and so on. In other words, an excess in the exchange of *Ribawi* goods within a single genus. The concept of *Riba Al-Fadl* refers to sale transactions while **Riba Al-Nasiah** refers to loan transactions.

Riba Al-Nasiah: '*Riba* of delay' is due to an exchange not being immediate with or without excess in one of the counter-values. It is an increment on the principal of a loan or debt payable, and refers to the practice of lending money for any length of time on the understanding that the borrower will return to the lender, at the end of the period, the amount originally lent together with an increase on it, in consideration of the lender having granted him time to pay. Interest, in all modern conventional banking transactions, falls under the purview of *Riba Al-Nasiah*. As money in the present banking system is exchanged for money with excess and delay, it falls under the definition of *riba*. There is a general accord reached among scholars that *riba* is prohibited under **Sharia'a** law.

al-sani': The ultimate seller in an Istisna'a contract.

Sadaqah: Deeds of giving, charitable donations, alms and so on.

Sahib-ul-Mal: Under the **Mudaraba Takaful** model, the entrepreneur (or **Mudarib** – the **Takaful** operator) accepts payment of the **Takaful** instalments or **Takaful** contributions premium (termed the **Ras ul Mall**) from investors or providers of capital or fund (**Takaful** participants) acting as *Sahib-ul-Mal*.

Salaf (loan/debt): Literally, a loan that draws forth no profit for the creditor. In a wider sense this includes loans for specified periods; that is, for short, intermediate and long term loans. *Salaf* is another name for **Salam** wherein the price of the commodity is paid in advance while the commodity or the counter-value is supplied in the future. Thus the contract creates a liability for the seller.

Salam: A contract in which advance payment is made for goods to be delivered later. The seller undertakes to supply some specific goods to the buyer at a future date in exchange for a price fully paid in advance at the time of contract. According to the normal rules of the **Sharia'a**, no sale can be affected unless the goods are in existence at the time of the contract. However *Salam* forms an exception, given by the Prophet, to the general rule provided the goods are defined and the date of delivery is fixed. It is necessary that the quality of the commodity intended to be purchased is fully specified leaving no ambiguity potentially leading to a dispute. The objects of the *Salam* sale are goods and cannot be gold, silver or currencies. The latter are regarded as monetary values, the exchange of which is covered under rules of **Sarf**, that is mutual exchange should be hand to hand (spot) without delay. With this latter exception, *Salam* covers almost everything capable of being definitively described as to quantity, quality and workmanship.

Sarf: Basically, in pre-Islamic times this was the exchange of gold for gold, silver for silver and gold for silver or vice versa. In **Sharia'a** law such exchange is regarded as sale of price for price (*Bai al Thaman bil Thaman*), and each price is consideration of the other. *Sarf* also means the sale of monetary value for monetary value, meaning foreign exchange transactions.

Sharia'a: The term *Sharia'a* has two meanings: Islamic Law and the totality of divine categorisations of human acts (Islam). *Sharia'a* rules do not always function as rules of law in the Western sense, because they include obligations, duties and moral considerations not generally thought of as 'law'. *Sharia'a* rules, therefore, admitting of both a legal and moral dimension, have as their purpose the fostering of obedience to Allah the Almighty. In the legal terminology, *Sharia'a* means the law as extracted by the **Mujtahid** from the sources of law.

Shirkah: A contract between two or more persons who launch a business or financial enterprise to make profits. In the conventional books of *Fiqh*, the partnership business may include both *Musharaka* and *Mudaraba*.

Sukuk: Islamic bonds, similar to asset-backed bonds.

Sunnah: Custom, habit or way of life. Technically, this refers to the utterances of the Prophet Mohammed other than the *Qur'an*, being known as the *Hadith*, or his personal acts, or sayings of others, tacitly approved by the Prophet.

Tabarru': A donation or gift, the purpose of which is not commercial but is given in seeking the pleasure of Allah. Any benefit that is given by one person to another without getting something in exchange is called *Tabarru'*.

Takaful: A *Sharia'a*-compliant system of insurance in which the participants donate part of, or all of their contributions, which are used to pay claims for damages suffered by some of the participants. The *Takaful* operator's role is restricted to managing the insurance operations and investing the insurance contributions.

Tamlik: Complete and exclusive personal possession. The act of giving, in a zakat sense, is only complete, from an Islamic perspective, if there is a full transfer of ownership of the *zakat* donation.

Tapir: Spending wastefully on objects that have been explicitly prohibited by the *Sharia'a*, irrespective of the amount of expenditure.

Wadia: System in which an Islamic bank acts as keeper and trustee of depositor funds.

Wakala: A contract of agency in which one person appoints someone else to perform a certain task on his behalf, usually against a certain fee.

Wakil: The agent appointed by the *Muwakkil* in a *Wakala* contract.

Waqf: An Islamic endowment in which a particular property is set aside, in perpetuity, for a particular charity.

Zakat: Literally, this means blessing, purification, increase or cultivation of good deeds. It is a religious obligation of alms-giving, on a Muslim, to pay 2.5% of certain kinds of wealth annually to one of the eight categories of needy Muslims.

Bibliography

This text draws on a wide variety of references. In order to appreciate the central elements that lie at the heart of Islamic banking, readers are strongly urged to consult the following *Sura* from the *Qur'an*. The key references to *riba* can be found in

- Sura 2: 275–280
- Sura 3: 130
- Sura 4: 161
- Sura 30: 39

BOOKS

Ahmad, Ausaf and Khan, Tariqullah (1997). *Islamic Financial Instruments for Public Sector Resource Mobilization*, Jeddah, Saudi Arabia: IDB, IRTI.

Ahmad, Ausaf and Khan, Tariqullah (eds) (1998). *Islamic Financial Instruments for Public Sector Resource Mobilization*, Jeddah, Saudi Arabia: IRTI.

Ahmad, Khurshid (ed.) (1976). *Studies in Islamic Economics*, Leicester, UK: The Islamic Foundation.

Al-Harran, Saad Abdul Sattar (1993). *Islamic Finance: Partnership Financing*, Selangor, Malaysia: Pelanduk Publications.

Al-Harran, Saad Abdul Sattar (1995). *Leading Issues in Islamic Banking and Finance*, Selangor, Malaysia: Pelanduk Publications.

Ali, Syed Ameer (1978). *The Spirit of Islam: A History of the Evolution and Ideals of Islam, with a Life of the Prophet*, London, UK: Chatto & Windus.

Ali, S. Nazim and Ali, Naseem N. (1994). *Information Sources on Islamic Banking and Economics, 1980–1990*, Kegan Paul International.

al-Misri, Ahmad ibn Naqid (1988). *Reliance of the Traveller: A Classical Manual of Islamic Sacred Law*, Translation by Nuh Ha Mim Keller: Amana Publications.

Al-Omar, Fouad and Abdel Haq, Mohammed (1996). *Islamic Banking, Theory, Practice and Challenges*, London, UK: Oxford University.

al-Qaradawi, Yusuf (1985). *The Lawful and the Prohibited in Islam*, Kuala Lumpur, Malaysia: Islamic Book Trust.

Archer, Simon and Karim, Rifaat Abdel (2002). *Islamic Finance: Innovation and Growth*, London, UK: Euromoney Books and AAOIFI.

Ariff, Mohammad and Mannan, M.A. (1990). *Developing a System of Islamic Financial Instruments*, Jeddah, Saudi Arabia: IDB, IRTI.

Armstrong, Karen (2002). *Islam: A Short History*, New York, USA: Modern Library (revised edn).

Ayub, Mohammad (2002). *Islamic Banking and Finance: Theory and Practice*, Karachi, Pakistan: State Bank Printing Press.

BenDjilali, Boualem and Khan, Tariqullah (1995). *Economics of Diminishing Musharakah*, Jeddah, Saudi Arabia: IRTI.

Bowker, John (1999). *What Muslims Believe*, Oxford, UK: OneWorld.

Burton, John (1990). *The Sources of Islamic Law: Islamic Theories of Abrogation*, Edinburgh, UK: Edinburgh University Press.

Burton, John (1994). *An Introduction to the Hadith*, Edinburgh, UK: Edinburgh University Press.

Chapra, M.U. (1985). *Towards a Just Monetary System*, Leicester, UK: The Islamic Foundation.

Chapra, M.U. (1992). *Islam and the Economic Challenge*, Leicester, UK: The Islamic Foundation.

Chapra, M.U. (2000). *The Future of Islamic Economics*, Leicester, UK: The Islamic Foundation.

Cook, Michael (2000). *The Koran: A Very Short Introduction*, Oxford, UK: Oxford University Press.

Cooter, Robert and Thomas Ulen (2000). *Law and Economics*, 3rd edition, Reading, MA, USA: Addison-Wesley.

Coulson, N.J. (1994). *A History of Islamic Law*, Edinburgh, UK: Edinburgh University Press.

De Lorenzo, Yusuf Talal (eds) (1997). *A Compendium of Legal Opinions on the Operations of Islamic Banks: Murabahah, Mudarabah and Musharakah*, London, UK: Institute of Islamic Banking and Insurance.

El-Gamal, M.A. (2003). *A Basic Guide to Contemporary Islamic Banking and Finance*, elgamal@rice.edu http://www.ruf.rice.edu/~elgamal

El-Gamal, M.A. (2003). *Financial Transactions in Islamic Jurisprudence*, Vols 1 and 2, Translation by Dr Al-Zuhayli: Kitaabun.com.

Esposito, John L. (1995). *The Oxford Encyclopedia of the Modern Islamic World*, 4 vols, Oxford, UK: Oxford University Press.

Farouqui, Mahmood (ed.) (1997). *Islamic Banking and Investment: Challenge and Opportunity*, Kegan Paul International.

Garrett, R. and Graham, A. (eds) (1998). *Islamic Law and Finance*, Introduction by William Ballantyne, London, UK: Graham & Trotman.

Hallaq, Wael B. (ed.) (2003). *The Formation of Islamic Law*, Aldershot, UK: Ashgate.

Haron, Sudin (1997). *Islamic Banking: Rules and Regulations*, Selangor, Malaysia: Pelanduk Publications.

Haron, Sudin and Bala Shanmugam (1997). *Islamic Banking System: Concepts and Applications*, Selangor, Malaysia: Pelanduk Publications.

Henry, C.M. and Rodney Wilson (eds) (2004). *Politics of Islamic Finance*, Edinburgh, UK: Edinburgh University Press.

Homoud, Sami Hassan (1985). *Islamic Banking*, London, UK: Arabian Information.

Homoud, S. (1985). *Islamic Banking*, London, UK: Graham & Trotman.

Institute of Islamic Banking and Insurance (1996). *Islamic Banking: An Overview*, London, UK: Institute of Islamic Banking and Insurance.

Institute of Islamic Banking and Insurance (2000). *International Directory of Islamic Banks and Institutions*, London, UK: Institute of Islamic Banking and Insurance.

International Association of Islamic Banks (1997). *Directory of Islamic Banks and Financial Institutions*, Jeddah, Saudi Arabia: International Association of Islamic Banks.

Iqbal, M. (ed.) (2002). *Islamic Banking and Finance*, Leicester, UK: The Islamic Foundation.

Iqbal, M. and Khan, Tariqullah (2005). *Financial Engineering and Islamic Contracts*, Basingstoke, UK: Palgrave-Macmillan.

Iqbal, M. and Molyneux, Philip (2005). *Thirty Years of Islamic Banking: History and Performance*, Basingstoke, UK: Palgrave-Macmillan.

Iqbal, Munawar and Llewellyn, David T. (2002). *Islamic Banking and Finance: New Perspectives in Profit Sharing and Risk*, London, UK: Edward Elgar Publishers.

Jaffer, S. (ed.) (2004). *Islamic Asset Management: Forming the Future for Sharia-Compliant Investment Strategies*, London, UK: Euromoney.

Kahf, Monzer and Khan, Tariqullah (1992). *Principles of Islamic Financing*, Jeddah, Saudi Arabia: IRTI.

Kamal, H. (2001). *Islamic Commercial Law: An Analysis of Futures and Options*, Cambridge, UK: Islamic Text Society.

Kamali, Mohammad Hashim (2000). *Principles of Islamic Jurisprudence*, Cambridge, UK: The Islamic Texts Society, revised edn.

Kettell, B. (1999). *Fed-watching: The impact of the Fed on the World's Financial Markets*, Financial Times-Prentice Hall.

Kettell, B. (1999). *What Drives Financial Markets?* Financial Times-Prentice Hall.

Kettell, B. (2000). *What drives the Currency Markets?* Financial Times-Prentice Hall.

Kettell, B. (2001). *Economics for Financial Market*, Butterworth's-Heinemann.

Kettell, B. (2001). *Financial Economics*, Financial Times-Prentice Hall.

Kettell, B. (2002). *Islamic Banking in the Kingdom of Bahrain*, Bahrain Monetary Agency (BMA).

Kettell, B. (2006). *Sukuk: a definitive guide to Islamic Structured Finance*, Thompson Hine.

Khan, M. Fahim (1996). *Islamic Futures and their Markets*, Jeddah, Saudi Arabia: IRTI.

Khan, Shahrukh Rafi (1988). *Profit and Loss Sharing: An Islamic Experiment in Finance and Banking*, Oxford, UK: Oxford University Press.

Khan, W.M. (1985). *Towards an Interest-Free Islamic Economic System*, Leicester, UK: The Islamic Foundation.

Lewis, Mervyn K. and Latifa M. Algaoud (2001). *Islamic Banking*, Cheltenham, UK: Edward Elgar.

Mehdi, Rubya (1994). *The Islamization of the Law in Pakistan*, Richmond, Surrey: Curzon Press.

Mills, Paul S. and John R. Presley (1999). *Islamic Finance: Theory and Practice*, London, UK: Macmillan.

Moore, Philip (1997). *Islamic Finance: A Partnership for Growth*, London, UK: Euromoney.

Rahman, Yahia Abdul (1994). *Interest Free Islamic Banking – Lariba Bank*, Kuala Lumpur, Malaysia: Al-Hilal Publishing.

Rosly, S.A. (2005). *Critical Issues in Islamic Banking and Financial Markets*, Bloomington, IN, USA: AuthorHouse.

Roy, O. (2004). *Globalised Islam, The Search for a New Ummah*, Huot & Co.

Saeed, Abdullah (1997). *Islamic Banking and Interest: A Study of the Prohibition of Ribā and Its Contemporary Interpretation*, 2nd edition, Leiden, The Netherlands: E.J. Brill.

Saleh, Nabil A. (1992). *Unlawful Gain and Legitimate Profit in Islamic Law*, 2nd edition, London, UK: Graham and Trotman.

Shirazi (1990). *Islamic Banking Contracts*, London, UK: Butterworth-Heinemann.

Siddiqi, M.N. (1983). *Issues in Islamic Banking*, Leicester, UK: The Islamic Foundation.

Siddiqi, M.N. (1985). *Partnership and Profit Sharing*, Leicester, UK: The Islamic Foundation.

Siddiqi, M.N. (1988). *Banking Without Interest*, Leicester, UK: The Islamic Foundation.

Udovitch, Abraham L. (1970) *Partnership and Profit in Medieval Islam*, Princeton, NJ, USA: Princeton University Press.

Usmani, M.T. (1998). *An Introduction to Islamic Finance*, Karachi, Pakistan: Idaratul-Ma'arif.

Usmani, M.T. (2000). *The Historic Judgment on Interest*, Karachi, Pakistan: Idaratul-Ma'arif.

Vogal, Frank E. and Samuel L. Hayes (1988). *Islamic Law and Finance: Religion, Risk and Return*, The Hague, The Netherlands: Kluwer Law International.

Warde, I. (2000). *Islamic Finance in the Global Economy*, Edinburgh, UK: Edinburgh University Press.

Zineldin, Mosad (1990), *The Economics of Money and Banking: A Theoretical and Empirical Study of Islamic Interest-Free Banking*, Stockholm, Sweden: Almqvist & Wiksell International.

AAOIFI PUBLICATIONS

AAOIFI (1999). *Statement on the Purpose and Calculation of the Capital Adequacy Ratio for Islamic Banks*, Manama, Bahrain: The Accounting & Auditing Organization for Islamic Financial Institutions.

AAOIFI (2002). *Accounting, Auditing and Governance Standards*, Manama, Bahrain: The Accounting & Auditing Organization for Islamic Financial Institutions.

AAOIFI (2002). *Investment Sukuk (Shari'ah Standard No.18)*, Manama, Bahrain: The Accounting & Auditing Organization for Islamic Financial Institutions.

AAOIFI (2003). *Shari'ah Standards*, Manama, Bahrain: The Accounting & Auditing Organization for Islamic Financial Institutions.

AAOIFI (2004). *Guiding Principles of Risk Management for Institutions* (Insurance companies offering only Islamic Financial Services), Manama, Bahrain: The Accounting & Auditing Organization for Islamic Financial Institutions.

AAOIFI (2004). *Capital Adequacy Standard for Institutions* (offering only Islamic Financial Services), Manama, Bahrain: The Accounting & Auditing Organization for Islamic Financial Institutions.

ARTICLES AND PAPERS

Abdallah, A. (1987). 'Islamic Banking', *Journal of Islamic Banking and Finance*, Jan–Mar, 4(1): 31–56.

Abdul, Majid and Abdul, Rais (2003). 'Development of Liquidity Management Instruments: Challenges and Opportunities', paper presented to the *International Conference on Islamic Banking: Risk Management, Regulation and Supervision*, held in Jakarta, Indonesia, 30 September–2 October 2003, organised by IRTI, Bank Indonesia and Ministry of Finance: Indonesia.

Abdul-Rahman, Yahla and Abdulah, S. Tug (1999). 'Towards a LARIBA (Islamic) Mortgage in the United States: Providing an Alternative to the Traditional Mortgages', *International Journal of Islamic Financial Services*, 1(2), Jul–Sep.

Aftab, M. (1986). 'Pakistan moves to Islamic banking', *The Banker*, June: 57–60.

Aggarwal, R.K. and Yousef, T. (2000). 'Islamic Banks and Investment Financing', *Journal of Money, Credit and Banking*, 32, 93–120.

Ahmad, Dr. Abdel Rahman Yousri (2001). 'Riba, its Economic Rationale and Implications', *New Horizon*, 109, May–June.

Ahmad, Ziauddin (1995). 'Islamic Banking: State of the Art', *IDB Prize Lecture*, Jeddah, Saudi Arabia: Islamic Research and Training Institute, Islamic Development Bank.

Alam, M.A. (2000). 'Islamic Banking in Bangladesh: A Case Study of IBBL', *International Journal of Islamic Financial Services*, 1(4), Jan–Mar.

Al-Bashir, M. and Muhammed al-Amine (2001). 'The Islamic Bonds Market: Possibilities and Challenges', *International Journal of Islamic Financial Services*, 3(1), Apr–Jun.

Al-Jarhi, Mabid Ali and Iqbal, Munawar (2001). 'Islamic Banking: FAQs', Occasional Paper #4, Jeddah, Saudi Arabia: Islamic Research and Training Institute.

Al-Suwailem, Sami (2000). 'Decision Under Uncertainty, An Islamic Perspective', in Islamic Finance: Challenges and Opportunities in the Twenty-First Century (Conference Papers). Loughborough: *Fourth International Conference on Islamic Economics and Banking*.

Anouar, H. (2002). 'Profitability of Islamic Banks', *International Journal of Islamic Financial Services*, 4(2), Jul–Sep.

Archer, S., Karim, R. Abdel and Al-Deehani, T. (1998). 'Financial Contracting, Governance Structures and the Accounting Regulation of Islamic Banks: An Analysis in Terms of Agency Theory and Transaction Cost Economics', *Journal of Management and Governance*, 2, 149–170.

Ariff, M. (1982). 'Monetary Policy in an Interest-Free Islamic Economy – Nature and Scope' in Ariff, M. (ed.). *Monetary and Fiscal Economics of Islam*, Jeddah, Saudi Arabia: International Centre for Research in Islamic Economics.

Ayub, Muhammad (1995). 'Meaning of Riba', *Journal of Islamic Banking and Finance*, 12(2).

Babikir, Osman Ahmed (2001). Islamic Financial Instruments to Manage Short-term Excess Liquidity, Research Paper No.41, 2nd edn, Jeddah, Saudi Arabia: Islamic Research and Training Institute.

Bacha, O.I. (1999). 'Financial Derivatives: Some Thoughts for Reconsideration', *International Journal of Islamic Financial Services*, 1(1), Apr–Jun.

Baldwin, K. (2002). 'Risk Management in Islamic Banks', in Karim, R. Abdel and Archer, S. (eds). *Islamic Finance: Innovation and Growth*, Euromoney Books and AAOIFI, pp. 176–197.

Basel Committee on Banking Supervision (BCBS) (2003). Consultative Document – Overview of the New Basel Capital Accord, Bank for International Settlements, April.

Bashir, A. (1996). 'Profit-sharing Contracts and Investment under Asymmetric Information', *Research in Middle East Economics*, 1, 173–186.

Buckmaster, Daphne (ed.) (1996). 'Central Bank Supervision: The Need for Unity', in *Islamic Banking: An Overview*, London: Institute of Islamic Banking and Insurance, pp. 143–145.

Buckmaster, Daphne, (ed.) (1996). 'Alternative Tools of Supervision by Central Banks', in *Islamic Banking: An Overview*, London: Institute of Islamic Banking and Insurance, pp. 146–150.

Chapra, M. Umer (1982). 'Money and Banking in an Islamic Economy', in Ariff, M. (ed.) *Monetary and Fiscal Economics of Islam*, Jeddah, Saudi Arabia: International Centre for Research in Islamic Economics.

Chapra, M. Umer (2000). 'Why has Islam Prohibited Interest?: Rationale Behind the Prohibition of Interest', *Review of Islamic Economics*, 9.

Chapra, M. Umer and Habib Ahmed (2002). Corporate Governance in Islamic Financial Institutions, Occasional Paper No. 6, Jeddah, Saudi Arabia: Islamic Research and Training Institute.

Chapra, M. Umer and Tariqullah Khan (2000). 'Regulation and Supervision of Islamic Banks', Occasional Paper No.3, Jeddah, Saudi Arabia: Islamic Development Bank – Islamic Research and Training Institute.

Cunningham, A. (2001). *'Culture of Accounting: What are the Real Constraints for Islamic Finance in a Riba-Based Global Economy?'* London, UK: Moody's Investor Services.

Dale, Richard (2000). 'Comparative Models of Banking Supervision', paper presented to the *Conference on Islamic Banking Supervision*, Bahrain: AAOIFI, February.

Dar, H.A. and Presley, J.R. (1999). 'Islamic Finance: A Western Perspective', *International Journal of Islamic Financial Services*, 1(1), Apr–June.

Dar, H.A. and Presley, J.R. (2000). 'Lack of Profit Sharing in Islamic Banking: Management and Control Imbalances', *International Journal of Islamic Financial Services*, 2(2), Jul–Sep.

El-Din, A.K. (1986). 'Ten Years of Islamic Banking', *Journal of Islamic Banking and Finance*, Jul–Sep, 3(3): 49–66.

El-Gamal, Mahmoud (2000). 'An Economic Explication of the Prohibition of Gharar in Classical Islamic Jurisprudence', in Islamic Finance: Challenges and Opportunities in the Twenty First Century (Conference Papers). Loughborough: *Fourth International Conference on Islamic Economics and Banking*.

Elgari, M. Ali (1997). 'Short Term Financial Instruments Based on Salam Contracts', in Ausaf Ahmad and Tariqullah Khan (eds.). *Islamic Financial Instruments for Public Sector Resource Mobilization*, Jeddah, Saudi Arabia: Islamic Research and Training Institute, pp. 249–66.

El-Karanshawy, Hatem (1998). 'CAMEL Ratings and their Relevance for Islamic Banks', paper presented to a Seminar on Islamic Banking Supervision, organised by the Arab Monetary Fund: Abu Dhabi.

El Sheikh, Fath El Rahman (2000). 'The Regulation of Islamic Banks by Central Banks', *The Journal of International Banking Regulation*, Fall, 43–49.

Errico, Luca, and Mitra Farahbaksh (1998). 'Islamic Banking: Issues in Prudential Regulations and Supervision', IMF Working Paper 98/30, Washington: International Monetary Fund.

Fadeel, Mahmoud (2002). 'Legal Aspects of Islamic Finance', in Archer, Simon and Karim, Rifaat Abdel (eds). *Islamic Finance: Growth and Innovation*, London, UK: Euromoney Books.

Gafoor, A.L.M. Abdul (2001). 'Mudaraba-based Investment and Finance', *New Horizon*, 110, July.

Gafoor, A.L.M. Abdul (2001). 'Riba-free Commercial Banking', *New Horizon*, 112, September.

Grais, W. and Kantur, Z. (2003). 'The Changing Financial Landscape: Opportunities and Challenges for the Middle East and North Africa', *World Bank Policy Research Working Paper* 3050, May 2003.

Haque, Nadeemul and Abbas Mirakhor (1999). 'The Design of Instruments for Government Finance in an Islamic Economy', *Islamic Economic Studies*, 6(2): 27–43.

Haron, S. and Norafifah Ahmad (2000). 'The Effects of Conventional Interest Rates on Funds Deposited with Islamic Banking System in Malaysia', *International Journal of Islamic Financial Services*, 1(4), Jan–Mar.

Hassan, Sabir Mohammad (2000). 'Capital Adequacy and Basel Guidelines: On Risk Weights of Assets for Islamic Banks', paper presented at the *Conference on the Regulation of Islamic Banks, in Bahrain, February*.

Hoque, M.Z. and Masdul Alam Choudhury (2003). 'Islamic Finance: A Western Perspective Revisited', *International Journal of Islamic Financial Services*, 4(4), Apr–June.

Ibrahim, Tag El-Din S. (1991). 'Risk Aversion, Moral Hazard and Financial Islamization Policy', *Review of Islamic Economics*, 1(1).

Iqbal, Zamir and Abbas Mirakhor (2002). 'Development of Islamic Financial Institutions and Challenges Ahead', in Archer, Simon and Karim, Rifaat Abdel (eds.) *Islamic Finance: Growth and Innovation*, London, UK: Euromoney Books.

Iqbal, Zamir (1997). 'Islamic Financial Systems', *Finance and Development (IMF)*, 34(2), June.

Iqbal, Z. (2001). 'Profit and Loss Sharing Ratios: A Holistic Approach to Corporate Finance', *International Journal of Islamic Financial Services*, 3(2), Jul–Sep.

Iqbal, Zubair and Abbas Mirakhor (1987). Islamic Banking, IMF Occasional Paper No.49, Washington: International Monetary Fund.

Iqbal, Munawar *et al.* (1999). *Challenges Facing Islamic Banking*, Jeddah, Saudi Arabia: IRTI, Occasional Paper #2.

Islamic Fiqh Academy of the Organization of Islamic Conference (1989). 'Islamic Fiqh Academy Resolutions and Recommendations', Jeddah, Saudi Arabia.

Kahf, Monzer (1998). 'Asset Ijara Bonds', in Ausaf, Ahmad and Khan, Tariqullah (eds), *Islamic Financial Instruments for Public Sector Resource Mobilization*, Jeddah, Saudi Arabia: IRTI.

Kahf, Monzer (1997). 'The Use of Assets Ijārah Bonds for Bridging the Budget Gap', in Ahmad, Ausaf and Khan, Tariqullah (eds.). *Islamic Financial Instruments for Public Sector Resource Mobilization*, Jeddah, Saudi Arabia: Islamic Research and Training Institute, pp. 265–316.

Kahf, Monzer (1996). 'Distribution of Profits in Islamic Banks', *Studies in Islamic Economics*, 4(1).

Kahf, Monzer (1994). 'Time Value of Money and Discounting in Islamic Perspectives Revisited', *Review of Islamic Economics*, 3(2).

Kahf, Monzer and Khan, Tariqullah (1992). *Principles of Islamic Financing*, Jeddah, Saudi Arabia: IRTI.

Karim, Rifaat Ahmed Abdel (2001). 'International Accounting Harmonization, Banking Regulation and Islamic Banks', *The International Journal of Accounting*, 36(2), 169–193.

Karsten, I. (1982). 'Islam and Financial Intermediation', *IMF Staff Papers*, March, 29(1), 108–142.

Khan, Mohsin and Abbas Mirakhor (1993). 'Monetary Management in an Islamic Economy', *Journal of Islamic Banking and Finance*, 10, Jul–Sep, 42–63.

Khan, Mohsin and Mirakhor, A. (1986). 'The Framework and Practice of Islamic Banking', *Finance and Development*, September.

Khan, Mohsin S. and Mirakhor, A. (1992). 'Islam and the Economic System', *Review of Islamic Economics*, 2(1): 1–29.

Khan, M. (1987). 'Islamic Interest-Free Banking: A Theoretical Analysis', in Khan, Mohsin S. and Mirakhor, Abbas (ed.). *Theoretical Studies in Islamic Banking and Finance*, Texas, USA: The Institute of Islamic Studies, pp. 15–36.

Khan, Mohsin S. (1986). 'Islamic Interest-Free Banking: A Theoretical Analysis', *IMF Staff Papers*, 33(1): 1–27, March.

Khan, M.Y. (2001) 'Banking Regulations and Islamic Banks in India: Status and Issues', *International Journal of Islamic Financial Services*, 2(4), Jan–Mar.

Khan, M.F. (1999). Financial Modernisation in the Twenty-First Century and Challenges for Islamic Banking', *International Journal of Islamic Financial Services*, 1(3), Oct–Dec.

Khan, M.F. (1991). Comparative Economics of Some Islamic Financing Techniques, Research Paper No.12, Islamic Research and Training Institute, Islamic Development Bank: Jeddah, Saudi Arabia.

Khan, Tariqullah and Ahmad, Habib (2001). Risk Management: An Analysis of Issues in the Islamic Financial Industry, Jeddah, Saudi Arabia: IRTI, Occasional Paper #5.

Khan, Tariqullah (1995). 'Demand for and Supply of PLS and Mark-up Funds of Islamic Banks – Some Alternative Explanations', *Islamic Economic Studies*, 3(1), Jeddah, Saudi Arabia: IRTI.

Khan, Tariqullah and Habib, Ahmad (2001). Risk Management: An Analysis of Issues in the Islamic Financial Industry, Jeddah, Saudi Arabia: IRTI Occasional Paper #5.

Maroun, Y. (2002). 'Liquidity Management and Trade Financing', in Karim, R. Abdel and Archer, S. (eds.). *Islamic Finance: Innovation and Growth* (pp. 163–175). Euromoney Books and AAOIFI.

Mirakhor, Abbas (1995). 'Theory of an Islamic Financial System' in *Encyclopaedia of Islamic Banking*, London, UK: Institute of Islamic Banking and Finance.

Mulajawan, D., Dar, H.A. and Hall, M.J.B. (2002). 'A Capital Adequacy Framework for Islamic Banks: The Need to Reconcile Depositors' Risk Aversion with Managers' Risk Taking', Economics Research Paper, 2–13, Loughborough University.

Naughton, S.A.J. and Tahir, M.A. (1988). 'Islamic Banking and Financial Development', *Journal of Islamic Banking and Finance*, 5(2).

Nienhaus, V. (1983). 'Profitability of Islamic PLS Banks Competing with Interest Banks: Problems and Prospects', *Journal of Research in Islamic Economics*, 1(1): 37–47.

Nienhaus, V. (1986). 'Islamic Economics, Finance and Banking – Theory and Practice', *Journal of Islamic Banking and Finance*, 3(2): 36–54.

Norman, A.A. (2002). 'Imperatives for Financial Innovation for Islamic Banks', *International Journal of Islamic Financial Services*, 4(2), Oct–Dec.

Obaidullah, Mohammad (1998). 'Capital Adequacy Norms for Islamic Financial Institutions', *Islamic Economic Studies*, 5(1–2).

Obaidullah, Mohammad (1998). 'Financial Engineering with Islamic Options', *Islamic Economic Studies*, 6(1), IRTI, IDB.

Obaidullah, Mohammad (1999). 'Islamic Financial Options: Potential Tools for Risk Management', *Journal of King Abdulaziz University (Islamic Economics)*. Saudi Arabia, 11, 3–28.

Obaidullah, Mohammad (2000). 'Regulation of Stock Markets in an Islamic Economy', Proceedings of the Third International Conference on Islamic Banking and Finance, August, Loughborough University, Leicester, UK.

Obaidullah, Mohammad (2001). 'Ethics and Efficiency in Islamic Stock Markets', *International Journal of Islamic Financial Services*, 3(2), Jul–Sep.

Obaidullah, Mohammad (2001). 'Financial Contracting in Currency Markets', *International Journal of Islamic Financial Services*, 3(3), Oct–Dec.

Obaidullah, Mohammad (2002). 'Islamic Risk Management', *International Journal of Islamic Financial Services*, 3(4), Jan–Mar.

Presley, John R. and Sessions, John, G. (1993). 'Islamic Economics: The Emergence of a New Paradigm', *Journal of Economic Theory*.

Qami, I.H. (1995). 'Regulatory Control of Islamic Banks by Central Banks', in Encyclopaedia of Islamic Banking and Insurance, Institute of Islamic Banking and Insurance: London, pp. 211–215.

Rahman, Y.A. (1999). 'Islamic Instruments for Managing Liquidity', *International Journal of Islamic Financial Services*, 1(1), Apr–Jun.

Rosly, A.R. and Sanussi, Mohammed M. (1999). 'The Application of Bay-al-Inah and Bai-al-Dayn in Malaysian Islamic Bonds: An Islamic Analysis', *International Journal of Islamic Financial Services*, 1(2), Jul–Sep.

Salehabadi, A. and Aram, M. (2002). 'Islamic Justification of Derivative Instruments', *International Journal of Islamic Financial Services*, 4(3), Oct–Dec.

Sarker, M.A.A. (1999). 'Islamic Business Contracts: Agency Problems and the Theory of Islamic Firms', *International Journal of Islamic Financial Services*, 1(2), Jul–Sep.

Sarwar, A.A. (1995). 'Islamic Financial Instruments: Definition and Types', *Review of Islamic Economics*, 4(1): 1–16.

Sundararajan, V., Marston, David and Shabsigh, Ghiath (1998). 'Monetary Operations and Government Debt Management under Islamic Banking', WP/98/144, Washington, DC: IMF, September.

Sundararajan, V. and Errico, L. (2002). 'Islamic Financial Institutions and Products in the Global Financial System: Key Issues in Risk Management and Challenges Ahead', IMF working paper, IMF/02/192, Washington: International Monetary Fund, November.

Udovitch, Abraham L. (1981). Bankers Without Banks: Commerce, Banking and Society in the Islamic World of the Middle Ages, Princeton Near East Paper No.30, Princeton, NJ: Princeton University Press.

Udovitch, Abraham (1970). Partnership and Profit in Early Islam, Princeton, NJ: Princeton University Press.

Uzair, Mohammad (1955). *An Outline of 'Interestless Banking'*, Raihan Publications, Karachi.

Uzair, Mohammad (1982). 'Central Banking Operations in an Interest-Free Banking System', in Ariff, M. (ed.).

Zaher, T. and Hassan, K. (2001). 'A Comparative Literature Survey of Islamic Finance and Banking', *Financial Markets, Institutions and Instruments*, 10(4): 155–199, November.

ALSO PUBLISHED BY THE AUTHOR

Islamic Finance in a Nutshell: A Guide for Non-Specialists, 2010, John Wiley & Sons, Ltd, Chichester.
Frequently Asked Questions in Islamic Finance, 2010, John Wiley & Sons, Ltd, Chichester.
Introduction to Islamic Banking and Finance, 2011, John Wiley & Sons, Ltd, Chichester.
Case Studies in Islamic Banking and Finance, 2011, John Wiley & Sons, Ltd, Chichester.
Islamic Capital Markets, 2009, available from the author.
Sukuk: a Definitive Guide to Islamic Structured Finance, 2008, available from the author.
Islamic Banking and Finance in the Kingdom of Bahrain, 2002, Bahrain Monetary Agency.

Financial Economics, 2001, Financial Times-Prentice Hall (translated into Chinese).

Economics for Financial Markets, 2001, Butterworth-Heinemann.

What Drives Financial Markets? 2001, Financial Times-Prentice Hall.

What Drives the Currency Markets? 2002, Financial Times-Prentice Hall.

Fed Watching: The Impact of the Fed on the World's Financial Markets, 1999, Financial Times-Prentice Hall.

The Valuation of Internet and Technology Stocks, 2002, Butterworth's-Heinemann.

The International Debt Game: a Study in International Bank Lending (co-author), 1985, Graham and Trotman.

A Businessman's Guide to the Foreign Exchange Market, 1985, Graham and Trotman.

Monetary Economics, 1985, Graham and Trotman.

Foreign Exchange Handbook, 1985, (co-author), Graham and Trotman.

Gold: An Analysis of its Role in the World Economy, 1982, Graham and Trotman.

The Finance of International Business, 1979, Graham and Trotman.

Index

Abu Bakr, 12
Accounting and Auditing Organisation for
    Islamic Financial Institutions (AAOIFI),
    79
accounting practices, *Sharia'a* compliant, 13
agricultural partnership, 96
Ahadith, 11, *see also Hadith*
Amanah (justice, faithfulness and trust), 121
Arbun (sale agreement), 121
Awqaf see Waqf

Bai' al-Dayn (sale of debt and receivables), 121
Bai' al-Muzayadah (sale and purchase
    transactions on auction and tender), 121
Bai' bil Wafa (sale of honour), 121
Bai' al-Istijrar, 121
Bai' Muajjal (credit sale), 121
Bai al-'inah (double sale), 121, 125
Bai Bithaman Ajil (goods sale on deferred
    payment basis), 121
Bank Muamalat, 111
banking with *Sharia'a* principles, 14

Council of Jurists (*Ulema* and *Fuqaha*), 12
counter value, 123, 125
current account, IBB, 121
    no interest, 8

Dhaman (guarantee), 122
Dayn (debt), 122
deposit, 30, 50
derivatives *see Maisir* (gambling)
Dubai Islamic Bank, 24
Duyun (debts), 122

faith, 1
family *Takaful*, 114, 118, 122
Faqih/Fuqaha (Muslim jurist), 111
fasting, 2
fatwa/fatawa (Islamic religious ruling), 30

Fiqh (Islamic law), 12–13, 15
Fiqh Academy, 101
Fiqh al-Mu'amalat (land and fruit trees lease),
    24, 122
fuqaha (Muslim jurists), 121

gharar (uncertainty), 112, 115
Al Ghunm bil Ghurm, 46, 59, 74, 86, 98

Hadith (sayings of Prophet), 2, 8, 11, 15–16
    see also Ahadith
Hajj (pilgrimage), 1–2, 8, 52
halal (permitted by *Sharia'a*), 122
haram (prohibited by *Sharia'a*), 122
Hawalah, 122
Hibah (gift and donation), 122

Ijara (leasing), 123–124
Ijara Muntahia Bittamleek, 77
Ijara wa Iqtina, 19, 77–79, 82–85, 122
Ijma' (consensus of opinion of learned men and
    jurists), 8
Ijtihad (effort), 11, 32, 122
imam (prayer leader), 1, 5–6, 12
'Inah (loan in sale form), 121–122
insurance, conventional *see* under *Takaful*
    (Islamic insurance)
International Islamic Insurance Company, 112
investment
    accounts, unrestricted, 50
    Sharia'a compliant, 15, 40
Islam
    see individual entries
Islamic banks
    gharar, prohibition of, 23, 27, 29, 105, 112,
      115, 122
    key principle activities of, 23–25
    profit and loss sharing, 23–24, 28, 31–32, 56
    riba, prohibition of, 23–24, 112
    risk-sharing, 116

Printed in the United States
By Bookmasters